THE RURAL COMMUNITY IN ANCIENT UGARIT

BY

MICHAEL HELTZER

1976

DR. LUDWIG REICHERT VERLAG · WIESBADEN

CIP-Kurztitelaufnahme der Deutschen Bibliothek

Heltzer, Michael

The rural community in ancient Ugarit.–1.
Aufl.–Wiesbaden : Reichert, 1976.
ISBN 3-920153-61-8

Gesamtherstellung: Allgäuer Zeitung Kempten
Printed in Germany

FOREWORD

This work was written with the generous financial support of the Israel Commission of Basic Research. The Faculty of Humanities of the University of Haifa contributed to the typing of the manuscript. The subvention of the Haifa University made possible the appearance of the monograph in print.

The author wishes to use this opportunity to express his deepest gratitude to all these institutions, whose generosity helped to bring the manuscript to the publisher.

My cordial thanks are also given to the publisher, Dr. Ludwig Reichert, and to Professor Dr. Richard Haase, whose aid and cooperation contributed so much during the editing of the manuscript.

M. Heltzer

TABLE OF CONTENTS

List of Abbreviations

AB	Analecta Biblica, Rome.
AfO	Archiv für Orientforschung.
AHW	*W. von Soden*, Akkadisches Handwörterbuch, 1959 —
ANET	*J. B. Pritchard*, Ancient Near Eastern Texts to the Old Testament, Princeton.
ANLR	Accademia Nazionale dei Lincei, Rendiconti della Classe di Scienze Morali, Storiche e Filologiche, Roma.
AOH	Acta Orientalia Hungarica, Budapest.
ArOr	Archiv Orientalny.
AS	Assyriological Studies, Chicago.
BA	Biblical Archaeologist.
BASOR	Bulletin of the American Schools of Oriental Research.
BiOr	Bibliotheca Orientalis, Leiden.
BM	Baghdader Mitteilungen.
BSOAS	Bulletin of the Schools of Oriental and African Studies, University of London.
BSSAW	Beiträge zur sozialen Struktur des Alten Vorderasien, Berlin, 1971.
CAD	Chicago Assyrian Dictionary.
CH	Codex Ḫammurapi.
Clar.	*L. R. Fisher* (ed.), The Claremont Ras Shamra Tablets, Rome, 1971.
CTC	*A. Herdner*, Corpus des Tablettes Cuneiformes Alphabétiques découvertes à Ras Shamra—Ugarit de 1929 à 1939, T. I et II, Paris, 1963.
CAH	The Cambridge Ancient History (Revised Edition).
DA	Dialoghi di Archeologia.
DISO	*Ch. F. Jean, J. Hoftijzer*, Dictionnaire des inscriptions semitiques de l'Ouest, Leiden, 1962–65.
FuF	Forschungen und Fortschritte (der deutschen Wissenschaft und Technik).
ILR	Israel Law Review.
IOS	Israel Oriental Studies.
JESHO	Journal of the Economic and Social History of the Orient, Leiden.
JAOS	Journal of the American Oriental Society.
JKF	Jahrbuch für Kleinasiatische Forschungen.
JNES	Journal of the Near Eastern Studies.
JNSL	Journal of the Northwest-Semitic Languages.
LAMMD	Lietivos TSR Aukstųjų Mokyklų Moksliniai Darbai, Istorija, Vilnius.
Levy	*J. Levy*, Neuhebräisches und Chaldäisches Wörterbuch über die Talmudim und Midraschim, I–IV, Leipzig, 1876–89.
Or	Orientalia, Rome.
OA	Oriens Antiquus.
OAC	Oriens Antiquus Collectio, Rome.
OLZ	Orientalistische Literaturzeitung.
PEFQS	Palestine Exploration Fund, Quarterly Statement.
PEQ	Palestine Exploration Quarterly.
PRU, II –	*Ch. Virolleaud*, Le palais royal d'Ugarit, II, Paris, 1957.
PRU, III –	*J. Nougayrol*, Le palais royal d'Ugarit, III, Paris, 1955.
PRU, IV –	*J. Nougayrol*, Le palais royal d'Ugarit, IV, Paris, 1956.
PRU, V –	*Ch. Virolleaud*, Le palais royal d'Ugarit, V, Paris, 1965.
PRU, VI –	*J. Nougayrol*, Le palais royal d'Ugarit, VI, Paris, 1970.
PS	Palestinskij Sbornik.

RA	Revue d'Assyriologie.
RAI	Rencontre Assyriologique Internationale.
RSI	Rivista Storica Italiana.
RSJB	Recueil Societé Jean Bodin.
SV	Sovetskoye Vostokovedeniye.
SY	Semitskiye Yazyki, Moscow.
U, V	Ugaritica, V, Paris, 1968.
UF	Ugarit-Forschungen, Neukirchen-Vluyn.
UT	*C. H. Gordon*, Ugaritic Textbook, Rome, 1965.
VDI	Vestnik Drevney Istorii, Moscow.
VT	Vetus Testamentum, Leiden.
WO	Welt des Orients.
WUS	*J. Aistleitner*, Wörterbuch der Ugaritischen Sprache, Berlin, 1963.
ZA	Zeitschrift für Assyriologie.
ZUL	*M. Dietrich, O. Loretz, J. Sanmartín*, Zur ugaritischen Lexikographie, VII, UF, V, 1973, pp. 79–104; VIII, UF, V, 1973, pp. 105–17; XI, UF, VI, 1974, pp. 19–38; XII, UF, VI, 1974, pp. 36–46.

LIST OF TABLES

INTRODUCTION

This book focuses on the village-community in the ancient kingdom of Ugarit during the fourteenth to thirteenth centuries B. C. What was the character of the community? What role did it play, particularly in the conduct of agriculture, the economic mainstay of the kingdom? What was the village-community's social structure?

The answers to these questions may shed light not only on the social and economic character of Ugarit, but also on that of Syria-Palestine in general in the Late Bronze Age. The study of this area as a whole has been hindered by the limited number of documents, apart from the Alalaḫ (Mukiš) texts. Even these texts do not yield information comparable to that found in the Ugaritic sources.

The sources available for this study were mainly the clay tablets written in alphabetic Ugaritic, in Akkadian cuneiform scripts, and in languages from the el-Amarna period and until the invasion of the "peoples of the sea" at the very beginning of the twelfth century B.C. and the destruction of the kingdom. These clay tablets are mainly administrative, economic, and legal documents from the royal archives. Some monographs and articles have been written about the social structure of ancient Ugarit in general,[1] but a major detailed investigation of the questions raised above does not exist. This author has contributed several papers concerning these questions,[2] most of which have appeared in Russian.

Concerning political history, we must base our conclusions on the brilliant works of *M. Liverani*[3] and *H. Klengel*,[4] except in those cases where examination of the sources forces us to reinterpret some minor events in the history of Ugarit. We are indebted to the French scholars, the late *J. Nougayrol*, and the late *Ch. Virolleaud*, for almost all text-editions. The sources edited by *Cl. Fisher*, and *A. Herdner* have also been of great importance.

---

[1] *A. F. Rainey*, A Social Structure of Ugarit, A Study of West Semitic Social Stratification during the Late Bronze Age, Jerusalem, 1967 (Hebrew with English summary); *M. Liverani*, Communautés de village et palais royal dans la Syrie du IIeme millenaire, JESHO, XVIII, 1975, No. 2, pp. 146–64; *M. Liverani*, La royauté syrienne de l'âge du Bronze Recent, "Le palais et la royauté," XIX Rencontre Assyriologique internationale, Paris, 1974, pp. 329–51.

[2] *M. Heltzer*, Problems of the Social History of Syria in the Late Bronze Age, OAC, IX, Roma, 1969, pp. 31–46; idem., The Economy of a Syrian City in the Second Millenium B. C., V International Congress of Economic History, Leningrad, 1970, separate paper, 13 pp. (with references to earlier papers).

[3] *M. Liverani*, Storia di Ugarit, Roma, 1962.

[4] *H. Klengel*, Geschichte Syriens im II. Jahrtausend v.u. Zeitrechnung, I–III, Berlin, 1965–70.

The Geographical and Environmental Setting

The territory of the ancient kingdom of Ugarit extended inland as far as forty to sixty kilometers from the Mediterranean coast. The northern border of the kingdom lay in the region of Jebel-el-ᶜAqra (Ugar. Mount *Ḫazi*, *Ṣpn* classical *Mons Casius*). Southward, the territory of Ugarit reached at least to Tell-Sūkas (ancient *Šuksi*). Thus, we can assume that the whole territory of the kingdom covered approximately 3,000–3,600 square kilometers.[5]

The capital city was situated close to the Syrian coast and about fifteen kilometers to the north of Latakije (ancient *Laodikeia*), where modern Ras-esh-Shamra (Ras-Shamra) is today. Not far from the tell is the bay of Minet-el-Beidha (White Bay, classical Leukos Limen, possibly in Ugaritian *Ma'ḫāzu*), the ancient harbour of Ugarit.[6]

The terrain was generally flat with occasional small hills. The only significant heights were those of Mt. Casius, in the northern part of the kingdom, which were covered with forests.[7]

Taking into account that except for some minor rivers in the area irrigation facilities were almost completely lacking, agriculture developed normally. The climate was relatively mild, as in most mediterranean countries. The rainfall on the coastal plain in modern times averages 800 mm., and sometimes even reaches 1500 mm.[8] Environmental conditions more favorable to agriculture were prevalent until the middle of the thirteenth century B.C., when climatic conditions reduced the amount of rainfall to the more or less modern average. Also, in ancient times the area was not completely deforested and this had a favorable influence on agriculture.[9] Still, Ugarit was much less densely populated than Meso-

---

[5] *K. Bernhardt*, Die Umwelt des Alten Testaments, Berlin, 1967, pp. 107–11; *G. Buccellati*, Cities and Nations of Ancient Syria, Roma, 1967, p. 38; *M. Astour*, Place-Names from the Kingdom of Alalaḫ in the North-Syrian List of Thutmose IV, JNES, XXII, 1963, pp. 220–41; *J. C. Courtois*, Deux villes du royaume d'Ugarit dans la vallée du Nahr el Kebir en Syrie du Nord, "Syria," XL, 1963, pp. 261–73; *J. Nougayrol*, Soukas-Shuksu, "Syria," XXXVIII, 1961, p. 215; *J. Nougayrol*, PRU, IV, p. 17; *H. Klengel*, Geschichte Syriens, III, Berlin, 1970, pp. 5–29.

[6] *M. Astour*, *Ma'ḫadu*, the Harbour of Ugarit, JESHO, XIII, 1970, No. 2, pp. 113–27.

[7] Cf. PRU, III, 11.700, where the concluding line of the lists states that the villages mentioned there are: 31) *âlāni* ᴰᴵᴰᴸᴵ*ḫuršāni*, "the settlements of the mountain (region)."

[8] Cf. *J. Weullersse*, Le pays des Alaouites, I, Tours, 1940.

[9] *M. Liverani*, Variazioni climatiche e fluttuaziani demografice nella storia Siriana, OA, VII, 1968, pp. 77–89; *M. Rowton*, The Woodlands of Ancient Western Asia, JNES, 26, 1967, pp. 261–77; ibid., The Topological Factor in the *ḫapiru* Problem, AS, XVI, pp. 375–87.

potamia and Egypt, where the economy was based on irrigation, resulting in a much greater agricultural yield.

We have no information about any large mineral deposits in the area of ancient Ugarit.

CHAPTER I

THE RURAL COMMUNITY

In Ugarit there were no rivers nor irrigation systems based on them. Still, the principal wealth of the kingdom was derived from agriculture and cattle breeding. It is natural to suppose that the peasants of Ugarit and their household, organized in village-communities, played a large role in the economic and social life of the country. Since most of our information is taken from the royal (palace) archives, we have a somewhat one-sided picture of the situation. Although there were certain "private" archives, (such as those of Rašapabu and Rap'anu, edited by J. Nougayrol in "Ugaritica" V). They belonged to royal scribes and functionaries and in large part they consisted of official documents taken from the royal archives.[1]

Social stratification in Ugarit becomes clear from the text PRU, IV, 17.238, written in the name of the Hittite king *Hattusilis III* to king *Niqmepa* of Ugarit. The Hittite king declares that:

3) *šum-ma arad šár* ^{mat}*Ú-ga-ri-it*	If a servant of the king of Ugarit,
4) *ù lu-ú mâr* ^{mat}*Ú-ga-ri-it*	or a son (citizen) of (the land) of Ugarit,
5) *lu-ú arad ardi šàr* ^{mat}*Ú-ga-ri-it*	or a servant of a servant of the King of Ugarit
6) *ma-am-ma i-te-eb-bi-ma*	(if) somebody (of them) rebels and
7) *a-na libbi*^{bi} *eqli* ^{amel}*ḫapiri* ^{il}*Šamši i-ru-ub*	enters the territory of the *ḫapiru* (people) of the Sun,[2]
8) *šarru rabû u-ul a-la-aq-qi-šu*	(I) the great king shall not accept him.
9) *a-na šàr* ^{mat}*Ú-ga-ri-it*	To the king of Ugarit
10) *u-ta-ar-šu*	I shall return him.

---

11) *šum-ma mâru*^{M} ^{mat}*Ú-ga-ri-it*	If the sons (citizens) of Ugarit,
12) *ša mâti*^{ti} *ša-ni-ti*	(who) are delivered for their
13) *i-na kaspi-šu-nu i-pa-aš-ša-ru*	silver (debts) to another country,
14) *iš-tu libbi*^{bi} ^{mat}*Ú-ga-ri-it*	and from the (land) of Ugarit
15) *in-na-ab-bi-it-ma*	they are fleeing,

[1] Cf. *M. Heltzer*, Review of "Ugaritica V," VDI, 1971, No. 1, p. 106 (Russian).

[2] The great Hittite king.

16) *a-na libbi*^{bi} ^{amel}*ḫapiri ir-ru-ub*	and entering the (territory) of the *ḫapiru,*
17) *šarru rabû u-ul a-la-qi-šu*	the Great King, I shall not accept him.
18) *a-na šàr* ^{mat}*Ú-ga-ri-it*	To the king of Ugarit
19) *u-ta-ar-šu*	I shall return him.

From this text we can see that in Ugarit there were three principal social categories or classes: "servants of the king," "servants of the servants of the king," and the "sons of Ugarit." The "sons of Ugarit" who had defaulted on their debts were, in certain cases, turned over to their creditors in foreign countries (cf. below pp. 57–58).

The text confirms that the king of Ugarit had sovereignty over the whole population of the kingdom. This was legally accepted by the Hittite king, to whom Ugarit was subservient. We also see that the text is dealing with originally free people, not slaves. The "servants of the king" and the "servants of the servants of the king" were those immediately dependent upon the royal authorities of Ugarit. The Ugaritic term designating them was *bnš mlk* "people of the king" (cf. below).[3] It is noteworthy that here, as in all the other texts concerned, the royal dependents *(bnš mlk)* are not identified with the main mass of the "sons of Ugarit." This is best seen in the text CTC, 71 (UT. 113) (cf. below pp. 19–21) where the number of bowmen conscripted to the army of Ugarit appears apart from the professional groups of royal dependents and also apart from fifty-nine villages of the kingdom of Ugarit. The same thing appears in PRU, V, 58 (UT. 2058): 1) *[spr] argmn špš* "[The list] of the tribute of the Sun" (i.e. the Hittite king), where seventy to eighty villages were mentioned together with the amount of their tribute. The reverse of the tablet gives the same tribute, which various groups of royal dependents *(bnš mlk)* had to pay.[4]

The term "sons of Ugarit" *(mârē*^{M} ^{al}*Ú-ga-ri-it)* is often used in reference to the inhabitants of the kingdom of Ugarit. In most cases similar wording appears in the texts, where, in addition to the "sons (citizens) of Ugarit," "sons" of the neighbouring kingdoms (*Siyannu, Amurru, Ušnatu,* etc.)

---

[3] *M. Heltzer,* "Royal Dependents" *(bnš mlk)* and Units of the Royal Estate *(gt)* in Ugarit, VDI, 1967, No. 2 (Russian with English summary), pp. 32–47; *M. Heltzer,* Problems of the Social History, pp. 43–46; *M. Liverani,* Storia di Ugarit nell'etá degli archivi politici, Roma, 1962, pp. 86–87; *G. Buccellati,* Cities and Nations, pp. 56–62; cf. also "Introduction," note No. 1.

[4] Cf. also the fragmentary tablet PRU, VI, 131 (RS. 19.35A), where the representatives of professional groups of the *bnš mlk* and residents of the villages are receiving arms, but the *bnš mlk* and villagers receive as separate groups.

are mentioned.[5] Designating the citizens of a country or the inhabitants of a local community as "sons" of that country or community is generally common to the whole ancient Near East. This forces us to conclude that the term "sons" refers to the main mass of the freeborn population, without special reference to social differences. In our case we have to pay special attention to the references to "sons" as inhabitants or citizens of certain local or rural (village) communities of the kingdom of Ugarit. For example, tablet PRU, IV, 17.288 relates a legal case between the king of *Ušnatu* and the "sons" of (the village) *Araniya* (cf. below). Here, as in many other places, we see that "sons" *(mârē)* were citizens of particular villages. We also learn that they were treated as a collective body in the legal and administrative senses.

[5] PRU, III, 16.270; IV, 17.43; 17.319; 17.234; 17.158; 17.341; 18.115; 17.239; 17.130; 17.79+374; 17.335+379+381+235; 17.397. Cf. also, *Buccellati*, Cities and Nations, pp. 36–38. Concerning other countries of the ancient Near East cf. *I. Djakonov*, Etnos i socialnoye deleniye v Assiri'i, SV, 1958, No. 6, pp. 45–56 (Russian with English summary).

CHAPTER II

TAXES AND DUTIES OF THE VILLAGES OF UGARIT

The Villages

Villages were usually, although not always, designated in the Akkadian texts of Ugarit by the term or determination sign URU-*âlu*. This corresponds to the Ugaritic word, *qrt* (pl. *qrit/qrht*) which appears in the alphabetic texts. The number of these villages may have reached 200, but it is possible that during almost two centuries of the existence of the late-Ugaritic kingdom several of the villages changed their name, several disappeared, and some new ones came into existence. It is also possible that the same villages sometimes appeared under different spellings. The exact number of villages is still unknown to us.

Table 1 lists the villages whose names were found in the documentary sources. Place-names are included only if a) the word *âlu* appears at least once before the name or the text deals in general with *âlu/qrit* of the kingdom, b) information is available about a collective duty or obligation of this village, c) the place-name is mentioned in a list where other known villages are mentioned. The names of the villages are listed according to the order of letters in the Ugaritic alphabet, as determined from the school tablets from Ugarit.[1] Names of well-recognized non-Ugaritic villages are omitted.

---

[1] *Ch. Virolleaud*, PRU, II, 184 (A. 12.63); 185 (B. 10.087); 186 (C. 15.71); 188 (19.40); *Gordon*, UT, p. 299, No. 1184; *O. Eissfeldt*, Ein Beleg für die Buchstabenfolge unseres Alphabets aus dem Vierzehnten Jahrhundert v. Chr., FuF, XXV, 1950, p. 217.

Table No. 1

		âlu/qrit—villages fulfilling collective tax, labor, and military obligations.	Border villages of the kingdom of Ugarit.[1]	Villages territorially encompassing sanctuaries and temple lands.[2]	Villages territorially encompassing "royal fields" *(eqil šarri)*.[3]	*gt*—villages territorially encompassing royal presses, stores of agricultural products and centers of the royal estate.[4]	Villages territorially encompassing royal lands, given into conditional landholdings by the king.[5]	"Royal dependents" *(bnš mlk)* residing in the village.[6]	Data about local administration or selfgovernment.
1	2	3	4	5	6	7	8	9	10
1.	*Agm* (^{al}*A-gi-mu*)[7]	+	—	—	—	+	—	+	—
2.	*Agn* (^{al}*A-ga-nu*)	+	—	—	—	—	—	+	—
3.	*Ayly* (*E-la-ya?*)[8]	+	—	—	—	—	+	+	—
4.	*Alḫb*	—	—	—	—	+	+	+	—
5.	^{al}*Al-lu-ul-lu*	—	+	—	—	—	—	—	—
6.	*Amḏy* (^{al}*Am-me-ša, A-me-za*)	+	—	—	—	—	—	+	—
7.	*Anan*	—	—	—	—	—	—	+	—
8.	*Ap*	+	—	—	—	—	—	—	—
9.	*Aps(nt)* (^{al}*Ap-su-na*)	+	—	—	—	+	—	+	+
10.	*Ar*[9]	+	—	—	—	—	+	+	+
11.	*Ary* (^{al}*A-ri*)[9]	+	—	+	—	—	+	+	—
12.	^{al}*Ar-ma-nu*	—	—	—	—	—	—	—	+
13.	*Arn(y)* (^{al}*A-ra-ni-ya*)	+	—	+	—	—	—	+	+

Table Nr. 1 continued

1	2	3	4	5	6	7	8	9	10
14.	*Arsp(y)*	—	—	—	—	—	—	+(?)	—
15.	*Arr(?)*	—	—	—	—	?	—	?	—
16.	*Art* (*^{al}A-ru-tu*)[10]	+	+	+	+	+	+	+	+
17.	*^{al}Ašri-Ba'alu*	+	—	?	—	—	—	—	+
18.	*Aǵt* (*^{al}A-ḫa-tu*)[11]	+	—	—	—	—	—	—	+
19.	*Atlg* (*^{al}A-tal-lig*)	+	+	—	—	+	+	+	+
20.	*^{al}Be-ka-ni*[12]	+	—	—	—	+	+	+	—
21.	*^{al}Be-ka-^{il}Ištar*[12]	+	—	—	—	—	—	—	—
22.	*Bly*	+	—	—	—	—	+	+	—
23.	*Bṣr(y)* *^{al}Ba-ṣi-ri*[13]	+	—	—	—	—	+	+	—
24.	*Bq^{c}t* (*^{al}Ba-aq-at*), *Ba-qa-at*)	+	+	—	—	—	—	+	—
25.	*^{al}Bi-ta-ḫu-li-wi*[14]	—	+	—	—	—	—	—	—
26.	*Bir* (*^{al}Bêru*, *Be-e-ru*)	+	—	—	—	+	+	+	+
27.	*Gb^{c}l/Gbl* (*^{al}Gi-ba-la*, *^{al}Gi-^{il}Ba'ala^{la}*)[15]	+	+	+	—	—	+	+	—
28.	*Gwl* (*^{al}Ga-wa-lu*)	—	—	—	+	+	+	+	—
29.	*^{al}Gal-ba*	—	—	—	—	—	—	—	—
30.	*Glbt* (*^{al}Gul-ba-tu*)[16]	+	+	—	—	—	—	—	—
31.	*Gll.Tky/Tky* (*^{al}Ga-li-li-tu-ki-ya*)[17]	+	—	—	—	+ ?	—	?	—
32.	*^{al}Ga-mil-tu*	—	—	—	—	—	—	—	—
33.	*^{al}Gan-na-na*[18]	+	—	—	—	—	—	—	—
34.	*Gn^{c}y*[18] (*^{al}Ga-ni-ya*)	+	—	—	—	+	—	+	—
35.	*Ḫbt/Ḫpty* (*^{al}Ḫu-ba-ta*, *Ḫu-pa-ta-u*, *Ḫuppatu*)[19]	+	—	+	—	—	+	+	+
36.	*Ḫlb* (*^{al}Ḫal-ba*)[20]	?	+	—	—	—	—	+	—
37.	*Ḫlby* (*^{al}Ḫal-ba-ya*)[20]	+	—	—	—	—	—	+	—
38.	*Ḫlb gngnt*	+	—	—	—	—	—	—	—
39.	*Ḫlb krd* (*^{al}Ḫal-bi qar-ra-di*)	+	—	—	—	—	—	—	—
40.	*Ḫlb ^{c}prm* (*^{al}Ḫal-bi ^{amelM}SAG.GAZ* (*ḫapiru*))	+	—	—	—	—	—	—	—

Table No. 1 continued

1	2	3	4	5	6	7	8	9	10
41.	*Ḫlb ṣpn* (^{al}*Ḫal-bi* ^{huršan}*Ḫa-zi*)[21]	+	—	—	—	—	—	—	—
42.	*Ḫlb rpš* (^{al}*Ḫal-bi rapši*)	+	—	—	—	—	—	—	—
43.	^{al}*Ḫu-ul-da*	—	—	—	—	+	+	—	—
44.	^{al}*Ḫu-lu-ri*	—	+	—	—	—	—	—	—
45.	^{al}*Ḫi-mu-lu*	—	+	—	—	—	—	—	—
46.	*Ḫmrn*[22]	+	—	—	—	—	—	—	—
47.	^{al}*Ḫe-en-zu-ri-wa*	—	+	—	—	—	—	—	—
48.	^{al}*Ḫa-ap-pu*	—	—	—	—	—	+	—	—
49.	*Ḫrbġlm* (^{al}*Ḫu-ur-ba-ḫu-li-mi*)[23]	—	+	—	—	+	—	+	—
50.	^{al}*Ḫar-ga-na*	—	—	—	—	—	—	+	—
51.	^{al}*Ḫu-ri-ka* (*ḪU*) *Iṣṣur-bêli*[24]	+	—	+	—	—	+	—	—
52.	^{al}*Ḫa-ar-ma-nu*	—	—	—	+	—	—	—	—
53.	^{al}*Ḫu-ur-ṣu-ú*	+	—	—	—	—	—	—	—
54.	*Ḫrṣb*c	+	—	—	—	—	—	+	+
55.	*Dmt/Dmt qdš(?)* ^{al}*Du-ma-tu, Du-mat-ya*[25]	+	—	—	—	—	—	+	+
56.	^{al}*Du-mat-qu, Du-ma-te-qi*[25]	+	—	—	—	—	—	—	—
57.	*Hzp*, ^{al}*Iz-pu*, ^{al}*Aš(?)-pi*[26]	+	—	—	—	—	—	+	—
58.	*Hry*	+	—	—	—	—	—	—	—
59.	^{al}*Wa-na-a-lum*	+	—	—	—	—	—	—	—
60.	^{al}*Zi-ib-ḫa*	+	—	—	—	—	—	—	—
61.	*Zbl*	—	—	—	+	+	—	—	—
62.	^{al}*Za-za-ḫa-ru-wa*	—	+	—	—	—	—	—	—
63.	*Zly* (*Zí-il-a*)[27]	+	—	—	—	—	—	+	—
64.	^{al}*Zi-im-ma-ri*	—	+	—	—	—	—	—	—
65.	^{al}*Za-mi-ir-ti*	—	+	—	—	—	—	—	—
66.	^{al}*Za-qi[XX]/Zi-qa-n[i]-ma*[28]	—	—	—	—	+	—	—	—
67.	*Zrn/Ẓrn* (^{al}*Za-ri-nu, Za-ri-ni-ya*)[29]	+	—	—	—	—	—	—	—

Table No. 1 continued

1	2	3	4	5	6	7	8	9	10
68.	*Ḫbš* (^{al}*E[.X.]iš*)[30]	+	—	—	—	—	—	—	—
69.	*Ḫdṯt*	+	—	—	—	+	—	—	—
70.	*Ḫl.ym*	+	—	—	—	—	—	—	—
71.	*Ṭbq/Tbq* (^{al}*Te-ba-qu*)	+	—	—	—	+	+	+	—
72.	*Yknᶜm* (^{al}*Ya-ku-na-mu, E-ku-naᶜamu*)	+	+	—	—	+	+	+	+
73.	^{al}*Ya-al-du*	+	+	—	—	—	—	—	—
74.	*Yny* (^{al}*Ya-na*)[31]	+	—	—	—	+	+	+	—
75.	*Yᶜly* (^{al}*Ya-a-lu*)	+	—	—	—	+	—	+	—
76.	*Yᶜny* (^{al}*Ya-a-ni-ya*)[31]	+	+	—	—	+	—	+	—
77.	*Yᶜrt/Yrt* (^{al}*Ya-ar-tu*)	+	—	—	—	—	+	+	—
78.	*Ypr* (^{al}*Ya-pa-ru*)	+	—	—	—	—	—	+	—
79.	*Yrgb*	—	—	—	—	—	—	—	—
80.	*Yrml*	—	—	—	—	—	—	—	—
81.	^{al}*Ya-ar-qa-nu*	—	+	—	—	—	+	+	+
82.	^{al}*Ya-at-ba*	—	+	—	—	—	—	—	—
83.	^{al}*Ku-um-bu*	+	—	—	—	—	—	—	—
84.	*Kmkty*	+	—	—	—	—	—	—	—
85.	^{al}*Ki-na-du*	—	+	—	—	—	—	—	—
86.	^{al}*Kan-g/ka-ki*	—	+	—	—	—	—	—	—
87.	*Knpy* (*Ka-an-na-pi-ya*)	—	—	—	—	+	+	+	—
88.	^{al}*Ka-an-za-ta*	—	+	—	—	—	—	—	—
89.	*Šbn/Ṯpn* (^{al}*Šu-ub-ba-ni*)[32]	+	—	—	—	+	+	+	—
90.	*Šdmy*	—	—	—	—	—	+	+	—
91.	^{al}*Šu-wa-u*	+	—	—	—	—	—	—	—
92.	*Šḥq* (^{al}*Ša-ḫa-iq*)	+	—	—	—	—	—	+	—
93.	^{al}*Šu-uk-si*[33]	—	+	+	+	—	—	—	—
94.	*Šlmy* (^{al}*Šal-ma*)	+	+	—	—	—	—	+	—
95.	*Šmg(y)* (^{al}*Šam-me-ga*)[34]	+	—	—	—	—	+	+	—
96.	*Šmngy*[34]	—	—	—	—	—	—	+	—

Table No. 1 continued

1	2	3	4	5	6	7	8	9	10
97.	*Šmny* (*^{al}Šam-na*)	+	—	—	—	—	—	+	—
98.	*^{al}Ša-ni-zu-la*	—	+	—	—	—	—	—	—
99.	*Šᶜrt* (*SÌG*)[35]	+	—	—	—	+	+	+	—
100.	*Šql* (*^{al}Šu-qa-lu*)	+	—	—	—	—	+	+	—
101.	*Šrš* (*^{al}Šu-ra-šu*)	+	—	—	—	—	—	+	—
102.	*Šrt*[36]	+	—	—	—	?	?	?	—
103.	*Šᶜt* (*^{al}Še-ta*)	+	—	—	—	+	—	+	—
104.	*Lbn(m)* (*^{al}La-ab-ni-ma ^{al}La-ab-nu*)	+	—	—	—	+	+	+	—
105.	*Liy*	—	—	—	—	—	—	—	—
106.	*Midḫ*[37]	+	—	—	—	—	+	+	—
107.	*Ma/iḫd*[37]	+	—	—	—	—	+	+	—
108.	*Mgdl(y)* (*^{al}Ma-ag-da-la*)[38]	+	+	—	—	—	+	+	—
109.	*^{al}Mi-ḫi/u*	+	—	—	—	—	—	—	—
110.	*Mḫr/Mǵrt*[39]	+	—	—	—	+	—	—	—
111.	*Mld*	+	—	—	—	—	—	+	—
112.	*Mlk* (*^{al}Mu-lu-uk-ku*)[40]	+	—	—	—	+	+	+	+
113.	*Mnt*	—	—	—	—	—	—	+	—
114.	*Mᶜbq*[41]	+	—	—	—	—	—	—	—
115.	*Mᶜbr*[42](?)	—	—	—	—	+	—	+	—
116.	*Mᶜqb* (*^{al}Ma-qa-bu, Ma-a-qa-bu, Ma-at-qab*)[41]	+	—	—	—	+	+	+	—
117.	*Mᶜr* (*^{al}Mu-a-ri*)	+	—	—	—	—	—	+	—
118.	*Mᶜrb(y)* (*^{al}Ma-'a-ra-bu, Ma-ra-bu, Ma-aḫ-ra-pa*)	+	—	—	—	+	+	+	+
119.	*Mṣbt* (*^{al}Ma-ṣi-bat, Ma-ṣa-bu(?)*)	+	—	—	—	+	—	+	—
120.	*^{al}Mi-ra-ar*	—	+	—	—	—	—	—	—
121.	*Mrat* (*^{al}Ma-ri-a-te*)	+	—	—	—	—	—	—	—
122.	*Mril* (*^{al}Ma-ra-ilu, Ma-ra-el*)[43]	+	+	—	—	+	—	+	—
123.	*^{al}Ma-ti-ilu*	—	—	—	—	—	+	—	—

Table No. 1 continued

1	2	3	4	5	6	7	8	9	10
124.	*Mtn*	—	—	—	—	—	—	—	—
125.	^{al}*Na-bal-ṭu*	—	—	—	—	—	—	+	—
126.	*Ndb(y) (*^{al}*Ni-da-bu/i)*	+	+	+	—	—	—	—	—
127.	*Nḫl(?)*	+(?)	—	—	—	+	—	—	—
128.	*Ngḫt (*^{al}*Na-ga-aḫ-tu)*[44]	+	+	—	—	+(?)	—	—	—
129.	*Nnu/i (*^{al}*Na-nu-u/i)*	+	+	—	—	—	+	+	—
130.	*Npkm/Nbkm (*^{al}*Na-ba/pa-ki-ma)*	—	—	—	—	+	+	+	—
131.	*Na-ap-ša-ti*[45]	—	+	—	—	—	—	—	—
132.	^{al}*Na-qa-bi*	+	—	—	—	—	—	—	—
133.	*Sknm (*^{al}*Šakna)*[46]	+	—	—	—	+	—	—	—
134.	*S_2ld (*^{al}*Su-la-du, Ṯlṭ/Ṯlṯ)*[47]	+	+	—	—	+	—	+	—
135.	*Slḫ*	+	—	—	—	—	—	—	+
136.	*Snr/Ṣnr (*^{al}*Si-na-ru)*[48]	+	—	+	—	+	+	+	—
137.	*Sġy*	—	—	—	—	+	—	—	—
138.	^{c}*nmk(y) (*^{al}*Inu-ma-ka-ya, Inu-ma-ka)*	+	—	—	—	—	+	+	—
139.	^{c}*nnky*[49]	—	—	—	—	—	+	+	—
140.	^{c}*nqpat (*^{al}*Inu-qap-at)*	+	—	—	—	+	—	+	—
141.	^{c}*r*	+	—	—	—	—	—	—	—
142.	^{c}*rgz*	+	—	—	—	—	—	—	—
143.	^{c}*rm(-t)*	+	—	—	—	—	—	+	—
144.	^{al}*Pu-gul-u/i*	—	+	—	—	—	—	—	—
145.	*Pd(y), (*^{al}*Pi-di)*	+	—	+	—	—	—	+	—
146.	^{al}*Pa-niš-ta-i*	—	+	—	—	—	—	—	—
147.	^{al}*Pa-ša-ra-te*	+	—	—	—	—	—	+	—
148.	*Ṣ*^{c} *(*^{al}*Ṣa-u, Š*^{c}*(?))*	+	—	—	—	—	+	+	+
149.	*Ṣ*^{c}*q (*^{al}*Ṣa-'a-qa)*	+	—	—	—	—	—	—	+
150.	*Qdš (*^{al}*Qi-id-ši)*	+	+	—	—	—	—	—	—

Table No. 1 continued

1	2	3	4	5	6	7	8	9	10
151.	*Qmy*[50]	+	—	—	—	—	—	+	—
152.	^{al}*Qi-am-l[a]*	—	—	—	—	—	—	?	—
153.	*Qmnz* (^{al}*Qa-ma-nu-zi*)	+	—	—	—	—	+	+	—
154.	*Qmṣ* (^{al}*Qi-mi-ṣu*)	+	—	—	—	—	—	+	—
155.	*Q(?)rn*	+	—	—	—	—	—	—	—
156.	*Qrt* (^{al}*KAR, Qu-ur-tu*)[51]	+	—	—	—	—	+	+	+
157.	*Rkb(y)* (^{al}*Ra-ak-ba*)	+	—	—	—	—	—	+	+
158.	^{al}*Ri-mi-šu*	+	—	—	—	—	—	—	—
159.	*Rqd* (^{al}*Ri-iq-di, Ra-aq-du*)	+	—	—	—	+	+	+	+
160.	*Riš* (^{al}*Rêšu, SAG.DU*)[52]	+	—	—	—	—	+	+	+
161.	*Ṯbil*[53]	+	—	—	—	—	—	—	—
162.	*Ṯlḥn* (^{al}*Si-il-ḫa-na*)	+	—	—	—	—	+	+	+
163.	*Ṯlrb(y)* (^{al}*Ša-lir$_{x}$-ba-a*)	+	—	—	—	—	+	+	—
164.	*Ṯm* (^{al}*Šum-me*)[54]	+	—	—	—	—	+	—	—
165.	*Ṯmry* (^{al}*Ša-am-ra-a*)	+	—	—	—	—	+	+	—
166.	*Ṯnᶜy* (^{al}*Šan-ne-a*)	+	—	—	—	—	—	—	—
167.	*Ṯnq* (^{al}*Šan-ni-qa*)	+	—	—	—	—	—	+	—
168.	*Ṯrmn*	+	—	—	—	+	—	+	—
169.	*Ġbl*[24]	+	—	—	—	—	—	—	—
170.	*Ġl/Ḫly* (^{al}*Ḫi-li, Ḫu-li*)[55]	+	—	—	—	+	+	+	—
171.	*Ġn* (^{al}*Ḫa-[n]i*)	—	—	—	—	—	—	+	—
172.	*Ġr*[56]	+	—	—	—	—	—	—	—
173.	^{al}*Tu-ḫi-ya*	+	—	—	—	—	—	—	—
174.	*Tkn*	—	—	—	—	—	—	+	—
175.	*Tmrm*	—	—	—	—	—	—	+	—
176.	^{al}*Tu-na-a-na*	—	—	—	—	—	—	+	—
177.	*Tpḥ*	—	—	—	—	—	—	+	—
178.	^{al}*Ta-ri-bu*	+	—	—	—	—	—	—	—

Table No. 1 continued

1	2	3	4	5	6	7	8	9	10
179.	*Trzy*	—	—	—	—	—	—	+	—
180.	^{al}*Tu-tu*	—	—	—	—	—	—	—	—
181.	^{al}*Ib-na-li-ya*	+	—	—	—	+	—	—	—
182.	^{al}*I-zi-ḫi-ya*	+	—	—	—	—	—	—	—
183.	^{al}*I-li-ya-me*	+	—	—	—	—	—	—	—
184.	*Ilštm*^{c} (^{al}*Il-iš-tam-'i*)	+	—	—	—	+	+	+	+
185.	*Ipṯl*	—	—	—	—	+	+	—	—
186.	*Irab*	+	—	—	—	—	—	—	—
187.	*Irbn*	—	—	—	—	—	—	+	—
188.	^{al}*Iš-qi*	—	—	—	—	—	—	+	+
189.	*Ubz/Ubš* (^{al}*U-bu-zu*)	+	—	—	—	—	—	—	—
190.	*Ubr*^{c}*(y)* (^{al}*U-bur-a*)	+	—	—	—	+	+	+	+
191.	*Ugrt*	—	—	—	—	—	+	+	—
192.	*Uḫnp* (^{al}*Uḫ-nap-pu*)[57]	+	—	+	+	—	+	+	+
193.	*Ull*	+	—	—	—	—	—	+	—
194.	*Ulm* (^{al}*Ul-la-mi*)	+	+	—	—	+	+	+	+
195.	*Uškn* (^{al}*Uš-ka-ni*)	+	—	—	—	—	+	+	+

---

[1] Based on information found in texts PRU, IV, 17.335 + 379 + 381 + 235; 19.81; 17.339A; 17.62; 17,366; 17.340 defining the borders of the kingdom of Ugarit.

[2] Cf. below pp. 71–74.

[3] Cf. below pp. 65–67.

[4] Cf. below pp. 29–30 and *M. Heltzer*, Royal Dependents . . ., VDI, 1967, No. 2, pp. 34–47; and ibid., review article on "Ugaritica" V, VDI, 1971, No. 1, pp. 113–17 (Russian).

[5] Cf. *M. Heltzer*, Povinnostinoye Zemlevladenye v drevnem Ugarite ("Conditional Land-holding in Ugarit"), LAMMD, IX, 1967 (1968), pp. 183–208 (Russian).

[6] Cf. below pp. 29–30 and *M. Heltzer*, Royal Dependents . . .

[7] On the identification of the Ugaritic spellings with the place-names written in Akkadian cf. PRU, II–VI, "Ugaritica" V and CTC; cf. also *A. M. Honeyman*, The Tributaries of Ugarit, JKF, II, 1951, No. 1, pp. 74–87 (partly out of date); concerning the general principles of the phonetic equivalents of the Ugaritic spellings and their interchanges, as well as their equivalent Akkadian spellings cf. *P. Fronzaroli*, La fonetica Ugaritica, Roma, 1955; *M. Liverani*, Elementi innovativi nell'Ugaritico non Letterario, ANLR, se. VIII, vol. XIX, 1964, fasc. 5/6; *M. Dietrich*,

O. *Loretz*, Untersuchungen zur Schrift und Lautlehre des Ugaritischen, (I), Der Ugaritische Konsonant ġ, WO, IV, 1968, No. 2, pp. 300–315; cf. also *M. Dietrich, O. Loretz, J. Sanmartin*, ZUL, VII, VIII, XI, XII.

⁸ PRU, VI, 29 (RS. 17.147), 5) *ša i-na eqlât*ᴹ *e-la-ya* "which is among the fields of Elaya."

⁹ Ar and Ary are different villages because both names appear several times on the same list of place-names (PRU, V, 40, CTC. 71 etc.). It is more difficult to differentiate between Ar and Ary in the texts written in Akkadian cuneiform: cf. ZUL, VII, pp. 82–84, No. 5–7.

¹⁰ ZUL, VII, p. 85, No. 9.

¹¹ Identification of *Aġt/Aḫatu* cf. *J. Nougayrol*, PRU, VI, p. 146; about the late Ugaritic graphic interchange, cf. note 7.

¹² *Bekani*, ᵃˡ*Be-ka-*ⁱˡ*Ištar* (nos. 20, 21) may be the same village, but this is impossible to prove.

¹³ ZUL, XI, p. 23, No. 21.

¹⁴ May be *Bi-ta-ḫu-li-mi;* cf. no. 49 *Ḫrbġlm* and the corresponding note 23.

¹⁵ Various spellings of the same place-name; the Akkadian spelling ᵃˡ*Gi-*ⁱˡ*Ba'ala* confirms that it cannot be identified with Byblos, always spelled *Gubla* in Akkadian texts from Ugarit, and sometimes appearing as *Gbl* in texts written in Ugaritic.

¹⁶ ZUL, VIII, p. 106, No. 17.

¹⁷ The text PRU, VI, 79 (RS 19.41) shows that at least at one time *Galilitukiya* belonged to the "cities of the (land) *Siyannu*" (26) *âlâni*ᴹ ᵐᵃᵗ*Si-e-a-ni*). *Galilitukiya* is also known as the name of an Ugaritic village and as such it had to perform certain obligations (PRU, V, 42. Tr, 2. *Gll.tky;* V, 18, 8 and 9 *Glltky*).

¹⁸ These two place-names may be spelling variants of the same village; another view cf. ZUL, XI, p. 23, No. 29.

¹⁹ Honeyman, The Tributaries, supposes that *Ḫpt* and *Ḫpty* are not identical. But it must be pointed out that the interchange b/p is normal for Ugaritic spelling. Also, *Ḫbt* and *Ḫpty* do not appear in the same list of place-names. Cf. Gordon UT, pp. 400 and 404, nos. 929 and 993, where an attempt is made to relate the place-name *Ḫbt* to the Hurrian goddess *Ḫeba(t)*, but the Akkadian spelling *(*ᵃˡ*Ḫu-ba-ta,* ᵃˡ*Ḫu-pa-ta-u)* contradicts this, cf. also ZUL, VIII, p. 109, No. 27.

²⁰ A comparison of the Akkadian spelling *Ḫalba* and *Ḫalbaya* confirms the supposition that these are two different place-names, cf. ZUL, VIII, p. 108, No. 24.

²¹ On *Ḫa-zi*//*ṣpn*, ZUL, VII, p. 97–98, No. 631–2.

²² It is uncertain whether this is a place-name or not.

²³ *Ḫrbġlm*—cf. PRU, V, 48. In text PRU, IV, 17.62, 15, Professor J. Nougayrol reads *Ḫu-ur-ba-ḫu-li-bi*—the Ugaritic reading helps to decipher as *mi*, cf. also C. Kühne, Mit Glossenkeil markierte fremde Wörter in akkadischen Ugarittexten, UF, VI, 1974, p. 166–167.

²⁴ Although Honeyman, The Tributaries, thinks that the ideogram *ḪU-Iṣṣuru* does not correspond to *Ḫu-ri-ka*, it is clear from PRU, III, 11.841 that ᵃˡ*Ḫu-ri-ka* performs its obligations together with ᵃˡ*Šu-ra-šu*. According to PRU, III, 10.044, 13, ᵃˡ*ḪU* performs its duties together with ᵃˡ*Šu-ra-šu* also. This suggests the identification of *ḪU* and *Ḫu-ri-ka* as spelling variants of the same village. *ḪU* is also *iṣṣuru* (bird) in Akkadian, thus ᵃˡ*Iṣṣur-Bêli* also seems to be identical with *ḪU* and *Ḫu-ri-ka;* cf. also ZUL, VII, s. 95, No. 63. The definitive clearing of the question demands new texts: may be *ġbl*//*ḪU-be-li*.

²⁵ ᵃˡ*Du-mat-qi* is possibly identical with *Dmt/*ᵃˡ*Du-ma-tu*. The autograph of the text PRU, VI, 138 (RS. 19.46) shows the spelling as ᵃˡ*Du-mat-ki*, which may be a rare usage in the Akkadian texts from Ugarit of the place-name determinative *KI* following the word. Thus, we may have to read the word ᵃˡ*Du-mat*ᴷᴵ.

²⁶ Cf. *Hzp* in PRU, V, 4, 28; 40, 43; 74, 31; 76, 16, etc. ᵃˡ*Iz-pi* in PRU, III, 11.

790, 24; 11.800, 5; U. V, 102 (RS. 20.207A, 13); PRU, VI, 70 (RS. 17.50), 11; 131 (RS. 19.35A); [al]*Aš(?)-pi* in PRU, III, 15.20, 4.

[27] Cf. *Zlyy* in PRU, II, 176, 3. Instead of the reading *Si-il-a*, of J. Nougayrol in PRU, III, 16.204, we would propose *Zi-il-a;* cf. ZUL, VII, s. 87, No. 31, where the Ugaritic and Akkadian spellings remain unidentified.

[28] U. V, 95 (RS. 20.011), 11 and U. V, 96 (RS. 20.12).

[29] This may be a respective change of *Z/Ẓ (Zrn/Ẓrn)*, as in the case of *Ṣnr/Zi-na-ru*. Interestingly, none of the texts containing lists of place-names mentions *Zrn/Ẓrn/Ṣnr/Z/Si-na-ru* in the same tablet. Thus, it may be that *Zrn/Ẓrn/Ṣnr* are identical.

[30] Strictly phonetically the Ugaritic *ḥ* had to be represented by the Akkadian *ē*.

[31] It may be that *Yny/Yᶜny* are identical; on this place-name, ZUL, VIII, p. 10, No. 29–30 *(Yny);* No. 35 *(Yᶜny).*

[32] Akkadian *š* = Ugaritic *ṯ* occurs frequently in personal and place-names; b-p interchange.

[33] Tell-Soukas, located south of Ugarit; cf. *P. J. Riis*, Sūkās, I, Kobenhavn, 1970.

[34] There may be various spellings of the same place-name *Šmg(y)/Šmngy*. Here, as a result of phonetic dissimilation, we have *n;* cf. also ZUL, VIII, s. 114–115, No. 3 (oben) und 3. *šmy*. 4. *šmgy*, und 3 (unten).

[35] *Šᶜrt* in PRU, V, 15, 25; 40, 11; 58, 12; 74, 11 etc; at the same time in PRU, III, 11.790, 4 as well as in Clar., 3, the Sumerian ideogram *SÍG* ([uru]*SÍG)* appears. *Šᶜrt* and *SÍG* both mean "wool" in Ugaritic and Sumerian respectively. So we have to identify the Ugaritic name with the Sumerian ideogram, as well as to reject the former reading of the village-name *SÍG* as *šipātu* ("wool" in Akkadian) by J. Nougayrol in PRU, III, 11.790, 4, and instead to propose the reading of *SÍG* as *Ša'artu*.

[36] The identity with *Šᶜrt* is not excluded.

[37] Different place-names.

[38] ZUL, XI, p. 31, No. 67.

[39] Only *gt Mġrt;* cf. notes 7 and 11.

[40] ZUL, XI, p. 33, No. 76.

[41] Possibly scribal error instead of *Mᶜqb(?)*.

[42] Possibly only a *gt;* cf. U. V, 96 (RS. 20.12), 7) *bît dim-ti Ma-ba-ri* 8) [al]*Šu-ba-ni*.

[43] ZUL, VIII, p. 112, No. 50.

[44] ZUL, XI, p. 33, No. 78.

[45] Cf. ZUL, XI, p. 33, No. 80.

[46] Identification based on the fact that the Ugaritic term *skn* and the Akkadian sumerogram *MAŠKIM-sākinu*, *šākinu* in Ugaritic are identical in meaning ("vizier," "governor"). Cf. *G. Buccellati*, Due noti di testi accadici di Ugarit, OA. II, 1963, *MAŠKIM-sākinu*, pp. 224–28; *A. F. Rainey*, [LÚ]*MAŠKIM* at Ugarit, Or., 35, 1966, pp. 426–28; cf., ZUL, XII, p. 43.

[47] The changes of s_2 in Ugaritic, whose phonetic value is not definitively clear, with *ṯ* and the syllable *su* (possibly read *šu*) in Akkadian, makes the identification possible.

[48] Cf. note 29.

[49] Possibly a scribal variant or error of *ᶜnmky;* on all the scribal variants of *ᶜnmky*, ZUL, VIII, p. 113–115, No. 57.

[50] ZUL, VIII, p. 115, No. 58.

[51] The general meaning of the word is "town," "dwelling," "village," but the lists of the collective obligations of the Ugaritic villages show that there was also a village with this name.

[52] [al]*Rêšu*, written by the ideogram *SAG.DU* in the Akkadian texts from Ugarit, formerly read by J. Nougayrol in PRU, III as [al]*Maḫsisu*. The comparison between

riš "head" and *SAG.DU* "head" forced us to propose the present reading (*M. Heltzer*, Povinnostnoye zemlevladeniye, p. 189, note 50) which is now also accepted by *J. Nougayrol*, PRU, VI, p. 147.

53 ZUL, VIII, p. 116, No. 66–67, akk. [al]*Ša-bi/pi-il.*

54 The spelling *ṯm* confirms the reading of the sign in Akkadian as *šum;* cf., ZUL, VII, pp. 82–3.

55 About the graphic interchange of *ġ/ḫ* cf. notes 7 and 11. Therefore it is impossible to agree with *P. R. Berger*, Zur Bedeutung des in den akkadischen Texten aus Ugarit bezeugten Ortsnamens *Ḫīlu (Ḫl)*, UF, II, 1970, pp. 340–46; cf., *C. Kühne*, UF, VI, 1974, pp. 166–167.

56 Cf., ZUL, XII, p. 40, No. 7.

57 Formerly read [al]*Aḫ-nab-bu*, without parallels in Ugaritic. Only the publication of PRU, V by Ch. Virolleaud in 1965 gave the alphabetic spelling *Uḫnp*. The Akkadian syllable *aḫ* can also be *uḫ; nab* and *bu* are also *nap, pu,* therefore there is no objection to the reading *Uḫ-nap-pu.*

Table No. 1 offers a more or less complete picture of the number of villages found in ancient Ugarit. Indeed, this number may be somewhat inflated since some villages may be listed more than once under different spellings. Few new place-names were revealed by the publication of new texts, beginning with PRU, V by the late *Ch. Virolleaud*, PRU, VI, "Ugaritica" V, and "The Claremont Ras Shamra Tablets."

The table shows that about 130 villages had to perform collective obligations and pay collective taxes. It is most interesting that all obligations were performed and paid collectively by the entire village. Thus, it is possible to clarify the communal character of such village-communities *(âlu/qrt)* and, even without the concrete data given below, to elucidate the collective responsibility of all members or families dwelling in such village-communities.

We will now consider the various duties, taxes, and other obligations of the rural communities.

Military Duty (conscription)

From the text CTC, 71 (UT, 113) we learn that professional groups of royal servicemen *(bnš mlk)* as well as certain villages, which were listed separately, had to supply a number of "bowmen"[2] to serve in some kind of guard unit. The text names sixty villages, of which fifty-five are legible.

2 Edge of the text: *ṭu[p]-pu ṣâbē*[M] *ša* [1][[§]*qašā]ti*[M], "tablet of bowmen." On the organization of the Ugaritic army, except for the bodyguard of the king, and without the data of PRU, VI, cf. *M. Heltzer*, Soziale Aspekte des Heereswesens in Ugarit, BSSAV, 1971, pp. 125–31.

The parallel text to CTC, 71, PRU, III, 11.841, is written in Akkadian.[3] We learn from these texts that various *âlu/qrit* had to send a number of men varying from one bowman on behalf of three villages[4] to ten bowmen on behalf of one village.[5] Most frequently we find 1–3 bowmen conscripted from a single village. The varying number of conscriptions was perhaps related to the population of each village.

In certain cases a "general conscription" of all or almost all male members of the rural community took place. It is even possible to compare the character of limited conscriptions, such as described in both texts mentioned above, with the character of "mass" or "general conscriptions" from the same villages.

Text CTC, 119 (UT, 321) is most interesting in this regard. It deals with the conscription of warriors from various villages of the kingdom and the number of bows (*qštm*, Akk. ^{iš}*qašātu*^{M}) and slings (*qlᶜ*, Akk. ^{mašak}*gabābu*) or shields[6] delivered to them. The tablet PRU, VI, 95 (RS. 19.74) also mentions a certain number of *ṣâbē*^{M} "soldiers" conscripted from various villages. A comparison of these texts gives us the following figures:

1. CTC, 71, 9 *Ẕrn*—1 bowman; PRU, VI, 95, 2 ^{al}*Za-ri-nu*—13 soldiers.
2. CTC, 71, 10 *Art*—1 bowman; PRU, VI, 95, 3 ^{al}*A-ru-tu*—13 soldiers.
3. CTC, 71, 11 *Ṯlḥny*—1 bowman; PRU, VI, 95, 7 [^{al}*Sil-ḫ*]*a-nu*—4[+x] soldiers.
4. CTC, 71, 12 *Ṯlrby*—1 bowman; PRU, VI, 95, 4 ^{al}*Šal-lir*$_{\text{x}}$*-ba-a*—10 soldiers.
5. CTC, 71, 13 *Dmt* (together with *Aǵt* and *Qmnz*)—1 bowman; PRU, VI, 95, 8 [^{al}*Du*]-[*m*]*a*-[*t*]*u*—x + [x] soldiers.[7]

---

[3] Although the beginning and the end of the tablet are broken, the correspondence of the names of the villages in both texts which deliver one bowman conjointly with another village shows that the text deals with the same kind of conscription (CTC, 71,49) *Agm w Ḫpty*—1—PRU, III, 11.841, 13–14) ^{al}*A-gi-mu*, *Ḫu-pa-ta-u*—1; (CTC, 71,58) *Ṣᶜ* and *Šḥq*—1; PRU, III, 11.841, 11—*Ṣa-a-qu* and *Ša-ḫa-iq*—1.

[4] CTC, 71, 13–15) *Dmt Aǵt w Qmnz*—1; 17–19) *Yknᶜm*, *Šlmy w Ull*—1; PRU, III, 11.841, 20–22) ^{al}*Uḫ-nap-pu*, ^{al}*Šu-ra-šu*, ^{al}*Ḫu-ri-ka*—1.

[5] PRU, III, 11.841, 15) ^{al}*Ma-a-qa-bu*—10, 22) ^{al}*Ra-aq-du*—10.

[6] Cf. Hebr. *qelaᶜ* "sling" and the parallels from other semitic languages—WUS, p. 227, No. 2413; UT, p. 478, No. 2233. The translation is not fully convincing since the texts of Mari employ for the term "sling," *aspu*, which corresponds to the Ugar. *utpt;* cf. *B. Landsberger*, Nachtrag zu *aspu* "Schleuder," AfO, XIX, 1959–60, p. 66. According to *Rainey* ("The Military Personnel of Ugarit," JNES, XXIV, 1965, p. 22), *qlᶜ* in Ugaritic could also mean "shield." *E. Salonen*, Die Waffen der alten Mesopatamier, Helsinki, 1965, p. 134, translated *k/gabābum* "Schleuder"—"sling," admitting that this word could also have the meaning "shield" (p. 135) and *(w)aspu(m)*, could have the meaning "sling."

[7] More than one without any doubt.

6. CTC, 71, 14 *Aġt* (together with *Dmt* and *Qmnz*)—1 bowman; PRU, VI, 95, 9 [a]l*A-ḫa-tu*—2 [+x] soldiers.
7. CTC, 71, 17 *Yknʿm* (together with *Šlmy* and *Ull*)—1 bowman; PRU, VI, 95, 10 [a]l*Y[a]-ku-naʿamu*—4 [+x] soldiers.
8. CTC, 71, 18 *Šlmy* (together with *Yknʿm* and *Ull*)—1 bowman; PRU, VI, 95, 6 [a]l*Šal-ma-a*—5 soldiers.
9. CTC, 71, 20 *Ṯmry*—1 bowman; PRU, VI, 95, 5 al*Šam-ra-a*[8]—6 soldiers.
10. CTC, 71, 21 *Qrt*—2 bowmen; PRU, VI, 95, 1 [a]l*Qa-ra-tu*—20 +[x] soldiers.
11. CTC, 71, 27 *Arny* (together with *Mʿr*)—1 bowman; CTC, 119—10 soldiers.[9]
12. CTC, 71, 57 *Mʿrby*—1 bowman; CTC, 119 *Mʿrby*—21 soldiers.[10]
13. CTC, 71, 21 *Ubrʿy*—2 bowmen; CTC, 119 *Ubrʿy*—61 soldiers.[11]
14. CTC, 71, 26 *Mʿr* (together with *Arny*, cf. above)—1 bowman; CTC, 119 *Mʿr*—6 soldiers.[12]

Text CTC also lists 21 men from *Ulm*,[13] 7 persons from *Bqʿt*,[14] 3 from *Ḫlb rpš*,[15] 3 from *Rkby*,[16] and 8 from *Šʿrt*.[17]

The text PRU, V, 16 (UT, 2016) 1) *Miḫdym* "people of (the village) *Miḫd*" apparently deals with the same subject. Only fifty names are legible, but the text originally listed no less than ninety people. The word *ḫlq* "perished" or "defected" appears after the names of the persons in I, 2, 4, 8, 9, 14 and II, 18.[18] This may indicate that we have here a conscription list or a text concerning a contingent designated for conscription.

The villages were listed in a particular order. We learn this by a comparison of texts CTC, 71 with PRU, VI, 95 and CTC, 119. In CTC, 71 the

---

[8] The reading of *J. Nougayrol*, PRU, VI, p. 88: al*Ú-ra-a*, but this town was situated in eastern Asia Minor and was known by its trade relations with Ugarit. Therefore, it seems correct to read the signs otherwise. The autograph of the text shows *ú* and the reading can also be *šam*. Thus, the reading *šam-ra-a* is preferable.
Ṯmry-Šamra occurs in various texts from Ugarit. (PRU, II, 181, 13; 81, 4; PRU, V, 44, 8; 58, II, 38; PRU, VI, 77, 7; 105, 2, 6, etc.)

[9] II, 1–12 named each personally.

[10] I, 25–48.

[11] CTC, 119, III, 1–46; IV, 1–19.

[12] CTC, 119, II, 13–20.

[13] I, 1–24, among them 12 *ġmrm*.

[14] II, 21–29.

[15] II, 34–37; cf. also PRU, II, 68 (UT, 162), 1–4 where the same three persons are listed.

[16] II, 35–39.

[17] II, 40–49.

[18] Cf. below with PRU, VI, 77 (RS. 19.32).

names of the villages listed in PRU, VI, 95 appear between lines 9–21. The names listed in CTC, 119 appear in CTC, 71 between lines 26–57. Possibly, these texts belonged to a very short chronological period. Nevertheless, they reveal a certain order of military conscription. Naturally, the larger conscriptions took place in times of emergency or warfare, and the given figures might include the whole militarily fit adult male population of the villages listed.

As mentioned above, CTC, 119 tells us about arms received from the royal stores by the conscripted villagers. Delivery of arms is listed in the tablet PRU, VI, 131 (RS. 19.35A) also. According to this text, bows *(ⁱˢqaštu)* and shields or slings[19] (ᵐᵃšᵃᵏ*ga-ba-bu* and ᵐᵃšᵃᵏ*iš-pa-tu*, Ug. *uṯpt* "quiver"(?)) were distributed to the various professional groups of royal dependents ("servicemen"—*bnš mlk*)[20] and to the villages, which are listed as single bodies. We find listed 7) ᵃˡ*Iz-pi*, 10) ᵃˡ*A-gi-mu*, 11) ᵃˡ*Ašar-*ⁱˡ*Ba'ali*, V, 1) ᵃˡ*Ilu-iš-tam-'i*. Each of them received 1–2 bows and 1–4 other pieces of armament.

By comparing texts CTC, 119 and PRU, VI, 95 with CTC, 71 and PRU, III, 11.841 we can see the difference between a partial and general conscription to the army of Ugarit. General conscription was a collective duty in which all villagers were obliged to participate. The royal authorities considered the village as one single body with collective responsibility. The term *ḫlq* "perished" or "defected" in PRU, V, 16 gives us good evidence of this. Nevertheless, it is clear that the people were personally free men, even though there was strict control by the state (royal) authorities. The data about the defection of villagers from their obligations (cf. below p. 58–62) lends strong support to this view.[21]

The peasants of the villages of Ugarit were also obliged to serve in the fleet of the kingdom. It is probably that only the coastal villages were obliged to perform such service. The available lists, however, may not contain the names of all the coastal villages which existed. We learn about conscription to the fleet from CTC, 79 (UT, 83). The people of various villages are designated by the term *bnšm* "people."[22]

---

[19] Cf. above, Note no. 6.

[20] Cf. also texts about receipt of various arms by royal dependents, PRU, V, 47 (UT, 2047), where *nqdm* "shepherds" are receiving bows *(qšt)*, slings and shields *(uṯpt, qlᶜ)* and spears *(mrḥ)*; cf. *Heltzer*, Soziale Aspekte . . . p. 130.

[21] At present we have no well-documented data about conscription activities, except partially *Alalaḫ* in Northern Syria, for the period of the second millenium b.c. Even the archives of Mari, with their enormous number of tablets have not yet produced adequate sources. Cf. *J. Sasson*, The Military Establishments at Mari, Rome, 1969.

[22] The manifold meaning of the term *bnš* cf. *M. Heltzer*, "Royal Dependents,"

1) *ṣb[u anyt]*	"Cre[w of the ship] (or "ships")
2) ^{c}*dn[ ]*	(of) ^{c}*dn[ ]* (p.n.)
3) *Ṭbq[ym x bnšm]*[23]	[People of] *Ṭbq,* [x men]
4) *M^{c}q[bym]*	[People of] *M^{c}q[b . . .]*
5) *tš^{c}, ^{c}[šr bnš]*	19 [men]
6) *Ġr*[24] *ṯ[. . . bnš]*[25]	*Ġr* x [men]
7) *ṣbu any[t]*	Crew (of the shi[p] (or "ships")
8) *bn Kṯan*	(of) *bn Kṯan*
9) *Ġr-- tš^{c}[^{c}šr b]nš*	*Ġr* 1[9 men]
10) *ṣbu any[t]*	Crew of the shi[p] (or "ships")
11) *bn Abdḥ[r]*	(of) *bn Abdḥ[r]*
12) *Pdym*	People of (the village) *Pdy*
13) *ḫmš bnšm*	five men
14) *Snrym*[26]	People of (the village) *Snr*
15) *tš^{c} bnš[m]*	nine me[n]
16) *Gb^{c}lym*	People of (the village) *Gb^{c}l*
17) *arb^{c} b[nšm]*	four m[en]
18) *Ṭbqy[m x bnšm]*[27]	People of (the village) *Ṭbq* [x men]."

As we see, the text mentions three ships, or three squads of ships under the direction of ^{c}*dn*, *Bn Kṯan*, and *Abdḥr*. The crews of these ships were conscripted from the villages *Ṭbq*, *Ġr*, *M^{c}qb*, *Snr*, *Gb^{c}l*, and *Pd(y)*. Members of the crews are always mentioned as *bnšm* and on this occasion it corresponds to the Akkadian term *mârē*^{M} ^{al}*X* "sons of the village (or city) x", i.e., the citizens of this certain community. Thus, we can determine

---

pp. 32–47; the previous full investigation of the text, *T. H. Gaster*, A Phoenician Naval Gazette, PEFQS, 1938, No. 2, pp. 105–21 is out of date. The restoration of the text is according to *A. Herdner* CTC.

[23] Our reconstruction; designate a certain number of people.

[24] May be a coastal town or village; cf. *M. Astour*, *Ma'ḫadu*, p. 113.

[25] Possibly *ṯn*—2; *ṯṯ*—6; *ṯlṯ*—3; *ṯlṯm*—30 etc.

[26] *Astor*, *Ma'ḫadu*, p. 115, a harbour village of the kingdom.

[27] Possible reconstruction.

[28] About the fleet of Ugarit in general cf. *J. M. Sasson*, Canaanite Maritime Involvement in the Second Millenium B.C., JAOS, 86, 1966, No. 2, p. 131; cf. also PRU, VI, 138 (RS. 19.46), where the lower fragmentary part of the text lists 16) ^{I}*Ib[ri]-mu-za* ^{al}*Du-mat*^{KI} 17) ^{I}*Id-ki-ya* ^{al}*Qar-ti-ya* 18) ^{I}*M[i-]nu-ru* ^{al}*Šal-mi-ya* 19) ^{I}*Ku-ru-e-[n]a* ^{al}*Ša-lir*$_{x}$*-bi-y[a]* (four persons from four various villages, and possibly similar listings in those parts of the text which were illegible of the text). This is followed by the summary: 20)*napḫar* 10 +*x ṣâbē*^{M} ^{iš}*elippi*, "in all, 10+x soldiers of the ship." Possibly, this text dealt also with the conscription to the fleet; on this text cf. also *A. F. Rainey*, Gleanings from Ugarit, IOS, III, 1973, p. 48.

that on certain occasions, or possibly even on a regular basis, people of certain villages were conscripted for service in the fleet of Ugarit.[28]

Non-military (?) Naval Service

The texts indicate that villages were not only obliged to serve in the navy but were obliged to participate in other maritime activities as well. To this end the authorities supervised the owners of all vessels of the maritime villages of Ugarit. Thus, the text CTC, 84 (UT, 319) is a list of "The vessels of the people of (the village) *Miḫd*" 1) *anyt. Miḫd[ym]*.[29] Although the text is in a bad state of preservation, we see that at least seventeen persons of *Miḫd*[30] possessed vessels of various types *(br, ṯkt, wry)*.[31]

More information on the same subject is revealed by the texts, PRU, V, 78 (UT, 2078) and PRU, V, 85 (UT, 2085). The location of these tablets upon their discovery in the tablet-baking oven gives the best evidence that they belonged to the very last period of the existence of the kingdom. PRU, V, 78 begins with the words 1) *Rišym qnum* "people of (the village) *Riš (the) qnum(?)*."[32] The text lists twenty-two persons by name, or the names of their fathers (*bn* x—"son of x"), or by both (x *bn* y). The text PRU, V, 85 lists at least fifteen persons (thirteen names are legible) by their own names and the names of their fathers. Every name is followed by the word *ṯkt*, which is the type of vessel owned by each person. In comparing both texts we gain the following results:

PRU, V, 78	PRU, V, 85
13) *Ilṯḥm*	5) *Ilṯḥm. bn. Dnn*
12) *Pss*$_2$	8) *Pss*$_2$*. bn Buly*
7) *bn. ᶜyn*	10) *Nᶜmn. bn. ᶜyn*
2) *bn Ilrš*	11) *ᶜpṯn. bn. Ilrš*
22) *Bn. S*$_2$*rn*	12) *Ilṯḥm. bn. S*$_2$*rn*
8) *bn. Grb*[32a]	13) *Šmlbu. bn. Grb*

[29] Our reconstruction contradicts *A. Herdner* (CTC) and *C. H. Gordon* (UT) *Miḫd[t]*.

[30] On the maritime position of *Miḫd* and *Riš* cf. *M. Astour*, *Ma'ḫadu*, pp. 115–16.

[31] About the types of vessels cf. *J. Sasson*, Canaanite Maritime Involvement, p. 131.

[32] *Dietrich, Loretz* and *Sanmartín* in ZUL, XI, p. 36, No. 101 give the interpretation of *qnum* as a personal name, but the real sense of the word may become clear from new text editions.

[32a] The reading of *Ch. Virolleaud* in PRU, V and *C. H. Gordon* in UT—*bn Grb[n]* is without foundation.

Thus we see that the owners of vessels who are named in PRU, V, 85 were also people of *Riš* who were obliged to perform some duty with their *ṯkt*-vessels.

We learn from the above sources that both the people of *Riš* and the people of *Miḫd* had to perform maritime duties[33] individually or collectively.

Labour obligations of the Villages

The Ugaritic *âlu/qrit* were obliged to work on various objects for the royal authorities (or the treasury) in different parts of the kingdom. The texts dealing with this obligation are PRU, III, 11.830 and 11.790,[34] PRU, II, 101 (UT, 1101), CTC, 65 (UT, 108), 66 (UT, 109), and 136 (UT, 84).[35]

From PRU, III, 11.830 and 11.790, as well as CTC, 65, we learn of forty-three villages which had to perform labour obligations. In general, they owed from 1–5 days of service. Eleven villages had to work more than five days; five of these owed more than ten days, and [al]*Be-ka-ni* was obligated to serve thirty days.[36]

CTC, 66 mentions "villages, which had to pay (to perform) the obligations in *Ṯlrby*" (1) *qrht. d. tššlmn.* 2) *Ṯlrbh*).[37] Eight villages are named whose people worked from fifteen days *(Mrat)* to two months *(Art)*. Most of the villages had to work "a month and five days."[38] Clearly, this text is dealing with relatively long periods of labour obligations. Perhaps the lengths of time mentioned were the total yearly obligations of the villages.

[33] Cf. PRU, V, 123 (UT, 2123) relating to vessels of various types in the hands of certain persons. However, the bad state of preservation of the tablet allows no further conclusions. Cf. also PRU, VI, 73 (RS. 19.107 A), a fragment listing people from at least three *âlu* and mentioning "ships" *([iṣ]eleppu)* at the end of the text.

[34] The efforts are counted in "days" *(ûmē[M])*, but this word is preserved only at the beginning of the text PRU, III, 11.830. Although in 11.790 the word *ûmē*[M] is not preserved, after [al]*A-me-za* and [al]*Gan-na-na* the same figures are written as in 11.830 (2 and 4, respectively). Following [al]*La-ab-ni-ma* the corresponding figures are 8 and 4, [al]*Mi-ḫi*—2 and 4, [al]*Ia-ar-tu*—5 and 4, [al]*Šu-ra-šu*, 7 and 4. It is thus possible to conclude that: a) PRU, III, 11.790 concerns corvée-labour, as does 11.830 also; b) the text are not contemporaneous and certain changes, due to chronology and demography, account for differing figures in both texts.

[35] Possibly PRU, V, 23 (UT, 2023) also. 1) *bnšm. dt. iṯ. alpm. lhm*, ("People who possess oxen"), possibly the following names are a list of the members of a rural community, together with their oxen, performing the labour-corvée. Cf. also PRU, V, 117 (UT, 2117), 1) *bnšm dt iṯ[. . .]* with personal names and figures following.

[36] PRU, III, 11.790, 4.

[37] UT, p. 491, No. 2424: *šlm*-Safᶜel ("to render service (or taxes)"). Cf. also I Krt 130 *ššlmt* ("peace gifts").

[38] *yrḫ. w. ḫmš. ymm* (i.e. no less than 33 days).

However, in only one instance can a direct comparison be made. This is in the case of the village of ^{al}*Ya-pa-ru* which is named in both texts. PRU, III, 11.830, 4 describes ^{al}*Ya-pa-ru* as carrying out its labour for eleven days, while according to CTC, 66 it did so for "a month and five days." Perhaps the shorter lengths of time related to a shorter period, for example, a season only. At the same time, these obligatory days may have been computed and recorded on the basis of the time it would take one man to perform all the obligatory days. Another possibility is that the different texts belong to different short periods of the history of Ugarit. In any case, it is definitely clear that the village as a whole had the collective responsibility for performing the obligatory labour.

The texts mentioned above do not make clear what type of labour was due. Sometimes it was certainly ploughing or some other work performed with pairs or oxen.[39] There also existed a mixed corvée consisting of labour and products produced by that labour. The relevant text in this regard is PRU, II, 10 (UT, 1010), which was elucidated by M. Dietrich and O. Loretz, who explained the difficult lines 5–6.[40] This text, which can be dated only in general, belongs to the XIV–XIII centuries b.c. It has the following wording:

1) *tḫm. rgm*	1) Say[41] the message
2) *mlk*	2) (of the) king
3) *l Ḥyil*	3) to *Ḥyil*[42]
4) *lm. tlik. ^{c}my*	4) Why[43] are you sending me (the question):
5) *iky. aškn*	5) How[44] shall I deliver

[39] PRU, II, 181 (UT, 1181), a badly preserved tablet, lists the villages *Gl[bt]*, *Dmt*, *Yrt*, *Ykn^{c}m*, *^{c}nmky*, *Qmnz*, *Ṯmry*, and 9 others, whose names are illegible. Following every village name "6 pairs of oxen in all" *(6 ta-pal alpē^{M} napḫaru)* is mentioned. Cf. also PRU, III, 15.114. According to this text the people of ^{al}*Šaknu* are freed from *šipru šarri* ("royal corvée") which they had to perform by: 14) *alpē^{M}-š[u-nu im]êrē^{M}-šu-nu* 15)*amêlē^{M}-[šu-nu]* ("[thei]r oxen, their [don]keys, [their] people").

[40] *M. Dietrich, O. Loretz*, Der Vertrag zwischen Suppiluliuma und Niqmad, WO, III, 1966, No. 3, p. 206. Also see *M. Dietrich, O. Loretz, J. Sanmartín*, Eine briefliche Antwort des Königs von Ugarit an eine Anfrage: PRU, II, 10 (= RS. 16.264), UF, VI, 1974, pp. 453–55; *E. Lipinski*, Une lettre d'affaires du chancelier royal, "Syria," L, 1973, pp. 42–49; *J. Hoftijzer*, A Note on *iky*, UF, III, 1971, p. 360.

[41] *rgm*. Cf. akk. *qibima*.

[42] Seems to be a functionary responsible for carrying out the royal order; concerning the name cf. *Lipinski*, p. 44, and UF, VI, p. 454.

[43] *lm*. Cf. UT, p. 428, No. 1384.

[44] *iky* cf. *Dietrich, Loretz*, "Der Vertrag," p. 206, and UF, VI, p. 453 which is in disagreement with the other interpretations.

6) ^{c}*ṣm. lbt. Dml*	6) tree trunks[45] for the sanctuary of *Dml?*
7) *pank. atn*	7) And I shall give[46]
8) ^{c}*ṣm. lk*	8) you the tree trunks:
9) *arb*^{c}. ^{c}*ṣm*	9) four tree trunks
10) ^{c}*l. Ar*	10) due from (lit. "on") (the village) *Ar*,
11) *w. ṯlṯ.*	11) and three
12) ^{c}*l. Ubr*^{c}*y*	12) due from (the village) *Ubr*^{c}*y*,
13) *w. ṯn* ^{c}*l*	13) and two due from
14) *Mlk*	14) (the village) *Mlk*,
15) *w. aḥd.*	15) and one
16) ^{c}*[l] Atlg*	16) due from (the village) *Atlg.*
17) *wl.* ^{c}*ṣm*	17) And (concerning) the tree trunks
18) *tspr*	18) you have to report[46a]
19) *n[r](?)n. al tud*	19) *N[r](?)n* (and) do not . . .
20) *ad. at. lhm.*	20) . . . .[47]
21) *ṯṯm. ksp*	21) sixty (shekels) silver.

Clearly this text is an order of the king for the delivery of tree trunks for the building or repair of the sanctuary of the deity *Dml*. It also seems that an individual by the name of *Ḥyil* was responsible for the project. The villagers of *Ar*, *Ubr*^{c}*y*, *Mlk* and *Atlg* had to cut and deliver the tree trunks, and this is generally understood by all the interpretors of the text, but we must point out its special significance for the social history of Ugarit. Possibly, it was an irregular corvée and therefore required a special order from the king. Thus, we see that maintenance of the sanctuaries was the responsibility of the royal authority. At the same time, villagers had to fulfill the corvée of cutting and transporting the tree trunks.

We know nothing about woodcutting corvée's in Mesopotamia. Such activities were more characteristic of the Syro-Phoenician coast. But the

[45] Cf. *Gordon*, UT, p. 356, No. 147, "how can I deliver logs ?" ^{c}*ṣm* is more probably understood as "tree trunks," cf. *Lipinski*, p. 42, "arbres"; UF, VI, p. 453 "die Hölzer."

[46] *Dml*—one of the Ugaritic deities. It is not clear why *Gordon*, UT, p. 385, No. 673, defines "*bt Dml*" as "a place name rather than a temple," at the same time giving in his glossary the name of the deity; *atn* "I shall give," UF, VI, p. 453, "ich bestimme," which is also acceptable for our interpretation.

[46a] According to UF, VI, pp. 454–55.

[47] The meaning is unclear; cf. UF, VI, p. 454, and *Lipinski*, pp. 42 and 46–48.

sources give us some opportunity to draw some analogies. The papyrus of *Wen-Amon* from the beginning of the eleventh century b.c., which tells of his voyage to Byblos, informs us that the ruler of Byblos "detailed 300 people and 300 cattle and he put supervisors at their head, to have them cut down the timber. So they cut them down."[48] (The story also tells about transporting tree trunks to the seashore, which is not characteristic of similar cases in Ugarit.) There is another text, from the Bible, dating from the middle of the tenth century b.c. which mentions a possible parallel.[49] This text deals with the stocking of timber by Hiram, king of Tyre and Sidon, for King Solomon. Unlike these two texts, the Ugaritic text is an official document concerning woodcutting in the mountainous coastal woodland of the Eastern Mediterranean. The woodcutters were the inhabitants of the rural communities performing their obligatory labour. It may well be that in Byblos at the time of the Wen-Amon, as well as in the time of Solomon, the labour force was recruited by the same means.

The cutting down and transporting of timber, according to the Wen-Amon text, required 300 people and 300 oxen, but the quantity of tree trunks was larger (II, 44–II, 58) than in the Ugaritic text, and the distance from the forest in the mountains to the seashore was longer. The text PRU, II, 10 mentions only ten tree trunks. The Wen-Amon text is valuable as an aid to understanding the duties of the villages of Ugarit since it is the first documentary account of a woodcutting corvée, not only in Ugarit, but as far as I know, in the whole ancient Near East.

In certain instances villagers were given special exemptions from service obligations.[50] These exemptions offer another demonstration of the existence of such labour obligations.

At the time of their obligatory labour the people of the village received food rations. CTC, 136 (UT, 84) relates 1) *Šlmym. lqḥ. akl* "People of *Šlm(y)* (^al^*Šalma)* took food." Eleven persons are listed who received from 1–3 *kd*—"jars"—of oil *(šmn)* each.[51] This lends support to the notion that everyone had to work a period longer than one day. We also see that

---

[48] *J. A. Wilson*, ANET, 1955, p. 28; cf. also the most recent edition of the papyrus, *M. A. Korostovtsev*, Puteshestviye Un-Amuna v Bibl, Moscow, 1960, p. 31, II, 42–44 (Russian).

[49] II Reg. 5,20.

[50] PRU, III, 16.188—King *Ammistamru* II frees a person (v, 6) *it-ti mâ[rē]*^{M} ^{al}*Ma-ra-ba-m[a?]* 7) ^{amel}*ka-al-la la-a il-la-a[k]* ("with the sons of Maraba *(Mᶜrb)* he must not go to the messenger (service)"). Cf. also PRU, 15.114, footnote 39.

[51] In Akkadian texts usually corresponded to *DUG* as a certain unit of liquid measure.

eleven people from the village were obliged to serve.[52] Text PRU, II, 59 (UT, 1059) also lists 1) *Maḫdym* "People of (the village) *Maḫd*". In lines 2–5 four persons are named and after each name is the word *lṯḥ*, a unit of dry measure. It is possible that here too the text is describing the distribution of products to people who were performing their service obligations away from their own villages.

Text U. V, 99 (RS. 20. 425) is a list of provision (wine and oil) deliveries for various professional groups of royal dependents of the kingdom of Ugarit. But among them also appear:

3) 1 *karpat karānu a-na mârē*ᴹ ᵃˡ*A-ri*
"1 jar of wine to the people of Ari"
4) 1 *karpat karānu a-na mârē*ᴹ ᵃˡ*Ul-la-me*
"1 jar of wine to the people of Ullame"

Thus, we see that in some cases food was distributed to the people of Ugaritic villages on an individual basis. This indicates that food was distributed only to those individuals who were working at any given time.

Text PRU, V, 79 (UT, 2079) from the tablet-baking furnace (i.e. from the last years of the existence of the kingdom of Ugarit) lists such a labor force.

1) *Rišym. dt. ᶜrb* 2) *b[.] bnšhm*	People of (the village) *Riš* who entered with their men
3) *Ḏmry. w. Pṯpṯ. ᶜrb* 4) *b. Yrm*	*Ḏmry* and *Pṯpṯ* entered with *Yrm*
5) *[Ily. w.]. Ḏmry. ᶜrb* 6) *b. Ṯbᶜm*	[*Ily* and] *Dmry* entered with *Ṯbᶜm*
7) *Ydn. bn. Ilrpi* 8) *w. Ṯbᶜm. ᶜrb. b. ᶜ[d]n*	*Ydn*, son of *Ilrpi* and *Tbᶜm* entered with *ᶜ[d]n*
9) *Ḏmry. bn. Yrm* 10) *ᶜrb. b. Adᶜy*	*Ḏmry*, son of *Yrm* entered with *Adᶜy*

Eight persons from *Riš* (citizens of *Riš*) appeared in four pairs. It seems likely that every pair appeared, together with one additional person, for the purpose of performing their obligatory labor together. The additional person may have been a dependent of the pair, or he may have been their slave. But there are also different views about the meaning of this text.[52a]

[52] We know that only 5 soldiers were conscripted from *Šlmy*/ᵃˡ*Šalma* (cf. above, p. 20).

[52a] *M. Dietrich, O. Loretz, J. Sanmartín*, Keilalphabetische Bürgschaftstexte aus Ugarit, UF, VI, 1974, s. 466 consider the text unhesitatingly to be a surety-grant.

Another text, U. V, 95 (RS. 20.01), gives additional data about obligatory service performed by people from the rural Ugaritic communities. This text must be a list of mixed character since it mentions not only villagers but also royal dependents *(bnš mlk)* of various royal *gt*, the primary units of the royal estate. The list includes people from various different villages. The text also gives information about the livestock possessed by the people whose names are listed in the tablet.[53]

1) ^{I}*Ya-ri-mu qa-du 5 napšātē*^{M}	*Yarimu* with 5 souls (people)
2) ^{I}*Ma-te-nu qa-du aššati-šu 6 alpū*^{M} 3) *ù* ^{I}*I-li-[y]a*	*Matenu* with his wife, 6 oxen and *Ili[y]a*
4) *4 napšātū*^{M} *[š]a* ^{I}*Ḫu-da-ši*	4 souls (people) of *Ḫudaši*[54]
5) *10 napšātū i-na* ^{al}*Uš-ka-ni 2 alpū*	10 souls (people) in (the village) *Uškani*, 2 oxen
6) $^{il}{}_{2}$*Ba'al-ma-te-ni qa-du 6 napšātē 2 a[l]pū 5(?) immer[ātu]*	*Ba'almateni* with 6 souls, 2 o[x]en, 5 she[ep]
7) ^{I}*Apteya 3 napšātū*^{M} *3 alpū*	*Apteya*, 3 souls, 3 oxen
8) ^{I}*Ni-qi-ma-du qa-du 6(?) napšātē-' 3 alpū*^{M} *13 [+2(?)] im[merātu]*^{M}	*Niqimadu* with 6 souls, 3 oxen, 13 [+2(?)] sh[eep]
9) ^{I}*Ili-*$^{il}{}_{2}$ *Ba'al [qa-du] 3*[55] *n[āpšā]tē*^{M} *24 [+x] immerātu 2 alpū*	*Iliba'al* [with] 3(?) s[oul]s, 24 [+2] sheep, 2 oxen
10) ^{I}*Maš-da-bi-ú 6 napšātē*^{M} *5(?) alpū 2 napḫar(?): 11*	*Mašdabiu*—6 souls, 5 oxen, in all(?) 11[56]
11) *Ya-ri-mu i-na* ^{al}*Za-qi-[xx]* ^{I}*Ilu-ra-[m]u i-na* ^{al}*Ḫa-[n]i* 12) ^{I}*Abdi-ili-mu i-na* ^{al}*Qi-am-l[a-a]*	*Ya-rimu* in (the village) *Zaqi[xx]* *Iluramu* in (the village) *Ḫani*[57] *Abdiilimu* in (the village) *Qiaml[a]*
13) ^{I}*Ili-ya-nu i-na dimti Gal-ni-um*	*Iliyanu* at the *dimtu*[58] *Galnium*

[53] Cf. the analysis of the text by *M. Heltzer*, VDI, 1971, No. 1, pp. 114–16 (Russian).

[54] Probably a scribal error—instead of ^{al}*Ḫu-da-ši* (cf. *Ḥdṯt*, PRU, II, 84 (UT, 1084), 11–12; 98 (UT, 1098), 22–23) we have the determinative of a masculine personal name.

[55] Or 6, the lower part of the text is damaged.

[56] A very strange summing up of people and cattle!

[57] Cf. *Ziqa-ni-ma* in table No. 1; *Ḫa-ni* Ug. *Ǵn*.

[58] Ug. *gt*, unit of the royal real estate; cf. *Heltzer*, VDI, 1971, No. 1, pp. 114–16.

14) *12(?) napšātē*^M *11 alpē*^M *3 imerū*^M *i-na dimti* ^I*Ilu-milki*	12 souls, 11 oxen, 3 donkeys at the *dimtu Ilumilki*[59]
15) *4 napšātē*^M *sa iṣ-ṣa-bat iš-t[u?] . . .]*	4 souls, who were seized fr[om . . . . .][60]
16) *1 amêlu i-na* ^al*Gi*$_2$-^il*Ba'ala*^lu	1 person in (the village) *Gibala*
17) *3 napšātē*^M *i-na* ^al*Ilu-iš-[t]am-i*	3 souls in (the village) *Iluiš[t]ami*
18) *[x+] 1 napšātē*^M *i-na* ^al*Pi-[d]i*	[x+] 1 soul in (the village) *Pi[d]i*
19) *1 [am]êlu i-na* ^al*Ḫal-ba-ya*	1 person in (the village) *Ḫalbaya*
20) *[x+] 2 napšātē*^[M] *4 napšātē*^M *[. . .] i-na* ^al*Tu-na-a-na*	[x+] 2 souls, 4 souls [. . .] in (the village) *Tunana*
21) *1 amêl[u i-n]a* ^al*SAG.DU(Riš)*	1 pers[on i]n (the village) *Rîšu*[61]

Lines 4–5, 11–12, 16–21 refer to people of various village-communities who had to perform labour obligations. This is confirmed by lines 13–14, where it is related that certain people had to perform their obligatory labour at the *dimtu/gt*, i.e. at the royal real estate in the kingdom of Ugarit. We also see that in the case which is dealt with by the given text various people had to work at the same time in different places. It is possible that a certain number of these people (line 15) were seized as defectors (cf. below p. 58–60). The villagers had to report for labor together with their beasts of burden, oxen and donkeys, although sometimes sheep are mentioned.

Despite the texts given here, the information about the distribution of obligatory labour inside the village-communities is relatively poor. Perhaps analysis of the families of the peasants inside the community can give us a more detailed picture of the distribution of the royal labour (cf. below Chapter VII, pp.90–96).

Payment of Taxes

Besides military conscription and the labour obligations mentioned above, which were distributed among the villages, there were also tax obligations in Ugarit. These taxes were paid by the village-communities in silver or natural products. We will first consider those taxes paid in silver.

[59] Not of the person *Ilumilki*, but it was the name of the *dimtu/gt*. Possibly, this dimtu was originally named after the former owner of the land.

[60] Possibly former defectors seized elsewhere for their royal corvée(?).

[61] Cf. table No. 1, note No. 52.

The sources mention "silver of the offerings" (or "offering people"—*kasap* ^{amelM}*šar-ra-ku-ti*/var. *širku*),[62] "silver of the honourables" *(kasap su-sa-pi-nu-ti)*,[63] and "silver" or possibly "fine" for scolding(?) *(kasap* ^{amelM}*zi-in-ḫa-na-še)*.[64] These specific taxes are only mentioned in regard to three villages (*Uḫnappu, Bi-i-ru,* and *E[. . .]iš*). The detailed lists of taxes which were paid in silver do not indicate the nature of the taxes.

It seems likely that there was no fixed sum due at regular intervals. The amount due varied from payment to payment. This can be seen from the comparison of two tax lists.

CTC, 69 (UT, 111)		PRU, II, 176 (UT, 159)	
1) *Qrt ṯqlm w nṣp*	(2.5 sheqels)[65]	1) *Dnt ṯlṯ*	(3 sheqels)
2) *Šlmy ṯql*	(1 sheqel)	2) *Qmnz ṯql*	(1 sheqel)
3) *Ary ṯql*	(1 sheqel)	3) *Zlyy ṯql*	(1 sheqel)
4) *Ṯmry ṯql. w. nṣp*	(1.5 sheqels)	4) *Ary ḫmšt*	(5 sheqels)
5) *Aǵt nṣp*	(0.5 sheqel)	5) *Ykn^{c}m ḫmšt*	(5 sheqels)
6) *Dmt. ṯql*	(1 sheqel)	6) *^{c}nmky ṯqlm*	(2 sheqels)
7) *Ykn^{c}m ṯql*	(1 sheqel)	7) *[Km]kt*[66] *^{c}šrt*	(10 sheqels)
		8) *Q(?)m šb^{c}t*	(7 sheqels)

According to CTC, 69, seven villages paid 8.5 sheqels. According to PRU, II, 176, eight villages paid 37 sheqels. The villages *Dmt, Ary* and *Ykn^{c}m* are mentioned in both texts and pay 1 and 3, 1 and 5, and 1 and 5 sheqels, respectively. It is not clear whether these were regular or exceptional payments. We cannot exclude the possibility that these lists may be excerpts from a more detailed tax list, or a memorial note, made by the scribe.[67]

Much more can be learned from the large tablet PRU, V, 58 (UT,

---

[62] PRU, III, 16.276, 9, from ^{al}*Uḫnappu;* PRU, III, 16.277—^{al}*Bi-i-ru;* PRU, III, 16.153, 13.

[63] PRU, III, 16.153, 13—^{al}*E[. . .]iš.*

[64] PRU, III, 16.244, 16, ^{al}*Bi-i-ri;* cf. also *I. Mendelsohn*, Samuel's Denunciation of Kingship in the Light of the Akkadian Documents from Ugarit, BASOR, 143, 1956, pp. 17–22.

[65] 1 Ugaritic sheqel varied between 9–9.9 grams, cf. the detailed study of *N. F. Parise*, "Per uno studie del sistema ponderale Ugaritico, DA, 1, 1970/71, pp. 3–36.

[66] Our reconstruction based on PRU, V, 119 (UT, 2119): 11) . . .*] Kmkty,* 12) . . .*] b Kmkty,* 16) . . .*] b Kmkty.*

[67] The fragment CTC, 70 (UT, 112) where at least 15 villages were listed (7 names are legible) seems to be a document of the same type. Following the place-names appears a number, varying from 1–10, for each village. *Hzp* has to pay *ṯn*—2; *Ḫrṣb^{c}-aḥd*—1; *Ypr arb*[^{c}]—4; *M^{c}qb. ^{c}šr*—10; *Ṯn^{c}y ṯlṯ*—3; *Ḫlb ^{c}prm. ṯn*—2, *Amdy. ṯlṯ*—3. These place-names do not appear in CTC, 69 and PRU, II, 176.

2058).[68] The obverse side is divided into two columns having a common heading: 1) *[spr]argmn špš*, "The list of tribute to the Sun" (i.e. the Hittite king).[69] In the first column 36–40 names were originally listed, but only 17 are fully legible or capable of reconstruction.[70] Every place-name is followed by number-signs, also only partly legible. The payments begin from 5 sheqels *(Ḫlb ^{c}prm, Qdš)* to 152 sheqels *(Ilštm^{c})* and in line 21, where the name of the village is damaged, the payment reaches 400 *(4 ME)* sheqels. The second column consisted originally of 40 place-names, but only 27 are fully legible or capable of reconstruction.[71] These payments vary from 4 sheqels *(Ḫlby)* up to 107 sheqels *(M^{c}qb)*, but the average seems to be less than 100 sheqels per village. On the reverse side of the tablet professional groups of the royal dependents, who had to pay the tax also, are listed. Text CTC, 71 concerning bowmen, mentioned above on pp. 18–19, offers new evidence that every village and every professional group was regarded as a single unit.

The total sum is written in Akkadian and only partly preserved. Although it does not aid in the reconstruction of the text PRU, V, 58 (UT, 2058) it is clear that the sum was paid in silver.[72] It is difficult to determine whether this was a regular or extraordinary payment. How-

---

[68] PRU, V, pp. 75–78, the editor, *Ch. Virolleaud*, gives only the autograph, transliteration of the lines, written in Akkadian on the reverse side, and the list of the Ugaritic villages and professional groups of royal servicemen *(bnš mlk)*—both incomplete. Despite the bad condition of the text, it is possible to reconstruct convincingly at least a part of the damaged lines.

[69] *argmn* ("tribute"), cf. *Ch. Rabin*, Hittite Words in Hebrew, Studies in the Bible, presented to M. H. Segal, Jerusalem, 1964, pp. 156–57 (Hebrew). Ugar. *argmn* corresponds to the hittite *arkamma(u)* ("tribute"); also *D. Pardee*, The Ugaritic Text 147 (90), UF, VI, 1974, pp. 277–78.

[70] Our reconstruction, which differs from the reading of *Ch. Virolleaud*, or is missing in his reconstruction, is marked by an asterisk (*): **Gb^{c}l, M^{c}rby, M^{c}r, Arny, ^{c}nqpat, Š^{c}rt, Ubr^{c}y, Ilštm^{c}, Šbn, Tbq, Rqd, *Šrš* (given also by *C. H. Gordon*), *[Ḫl]b krd, [Ḫl]b ^{c}prm, Qdš, Amḏy, *[Gn]^{c}y*.

[71] *M^{c}qb, Agm, Ḫpty, Ypr, Ḫrṣb^{c}, Uḫnp, Art, Nnu, Šmg, Šmn, Lbnm, Ṯrm, Bṣr, Midḫ, *Ḥlym [Ḫ]lby, ^{c}r, *^{c}n[mky]* (also in UT), *Glbty, Ykn^{c}m, Šlmy, *Ṯl[rby], Ṯm[ry], Aġ[t, Dm[t], *Šl[ḥny]* (cf. *Šlḥny*-table No. 1. Not *Šlmy* for the second time, as it is reconstructed by *C. H. Gordon*).

[72] Rev, II, 6) *[x l]i-im 1 me-at 22 + [x]* 7) *[ ]na[pḫ]ar kaspi^{M} 10 alāni^{M}* 8) *[x l]i-im 6 me-a[t] 30 [+x]* 9) *na[pḫ]ar kaspi^{M} al[āni^{M}]* (Dividing line follows). 10) *[x l]i-im* 56 *[+x]* 11) *[nap]ḫar kasp[i^{M}]*.

"6) [x th]ousand 122 [+x] 7) [] at [al]l silver [from] 10 villages 8) [x th]ousand 630 [+x] at [al]l silver (from the) vil[lages] (Dividing line) 10) [x th]ousand 56 [+x] 11) [at] all (sheqels of) silve[r].

Thus we see that after the listing of the professional groups there is the total sum collected from the âlu, and then the grand total including the professional groups; cf. also *Liverani*, Communautes, . . . p. 147, note 2.

ever, compared with other instances (for example, CTC, 69 and PRU, II, 171, where the village *Ykn^{c}m* had to pay 1 and 5 sheqels, respectively, and PRU, V, 58 where *Ykn^{c}m* had to pay 21 sheqels; and CTC, 69 and PRU, V, 58, where the village *Šlmy* had to pay 1 and 43+x sheqels, respectively), the payments mentioned above were much heavier than the norm. Perhaps the figures mentioned were payments made over a period of time longer than in the other texts. Or perhaps the tribute to the Hittite king was an extraordinary payment.

In connection with the taxes mentioned above the question arises: how were taxes collected? In our opinion, there is no data to confirm the view of N. B. Yankovska that merchants *(tamkars)* from abroad farmed the taxes in Ugarit.[73] Contrary to this view, the text PRU, V, 107 (UT, 2107), found in the tablet-baking furnace, provides convincing testimony that, at least in some cases during the last period of the existence of the kingdom of Ugarit, the village taxes were collected by *tamkars* of the king of Ugarit. The text reads as follows:

1) *spr argmnm*	List of the tribute-collectors[74]
2) *^{c}šrm. ksp. d. mkr* 3) *Mlk*	20 (sheqels) silver from the *tamkar* of (the village) *Mlk* (*^{a1}Mulukku)*
4) *ṯlṯ. mat. ksp. d. Šbn*	300 (sheqels) silver from (the *tamkar*) of (the village) *Šbn*
5) *mit. ksp. d. Ṭbq*	100 (sheqels) silver from (the *tamkar* of the village) *Ṭbq*
6) *ṯmnym arb^c* 7) *kbd ksp.* 8) *nqdym*	84— totally[75] (sheqels) of silver (from) the shepherds
9) *ḫmšm. lmit* 10) *ksp. d. mkr. Ar*	150 (sheqels) silver from the *tamkar* of (the village) *Ar*

[73] *N. B. Yankovska*, L'autonomie de la communauté a Ougarit (garanties et structure), VDI, 1963, No. 3, p. 33 (Russian). The contrary view is presented by *M. Heltzer*, Once More on Communal Self-Government in Ugarit, VDI, 1965, No. 2, pp. 11–12 (Russian).

[74] Or "tribute-deliverers" (to the treasury). This is the only case where the word *argmn* ("tribute") is used in the plural form *(argmnm)*. Perhaps there is a secondary noun from *argmn*, "the *argmn* collectors" or "the *argmn* deliverers." Possibly, this was also a tax for paying tribute to the Hittite king; *Pardee*, UF, VI, p. 277, does not explain the plural form *(argmnm)*.

[75] *kbd*, in various lists and economic texts from Ugarit, in the sense of "totally," but not necessarily summing up the results. Cf. *M. Liverani*, "*kbd*" nei testi amministrativi ugaritici, UF, II, pp. 89–108.

11) *arbʿm ksp dmkr*	40 (sheqels) silver from the *tamkar*
14) *Ilštmʿ*	of (the village) *Ilštmʿ*
15) *ʿšrm. l mit. ksp*	120 (sheqels) silver
16) *ʿl bn Alkbl Šb[ny]*	on[76] (or "to") *bn Alkbl*, man of (the village) *Šb[n]*
17) *ʿšrm ksp ʿl*	20 (sheqels) silver on (or "to")
18) *Wrt, Mtny. wʿl*	*Wrt*, man of (the village) *Mtn* and on
19) *Prdmy. aṯth*	*Prdmy*, his wife

This text shows that the tax was paid by six villages and one professional group of "royal men" *(bnš mlk)*—the shephers *(nqdm)*. The silver had to be collected by special *tamkars (mkrm)*, royal commercial agents[76a] who were undoubtedly dependents of the king of Ugarit. Every village, as well as every group of *bnš mlk*, was considered a single unit, and as such was collectively obliged to pay the tax imposed on the village or group. The tax farmer was obliged to see that this payment reached the royal treasury. At least at the very end of the existence of the kingdom, it is possible that the taxes were farmed out to the *tamkars* of the king of Ugarit.

Mixed taxes consisting of silver and natural products were also collected in Ugarit, although data concerning this matter is very scarse. We know of a certain pasture-tax *(ma-aq-qa-du)* which was paid in sheep.[77] We also know about a pasture-tax paid in silver, *kasap ša maqadu* "silver for pasture." This tax was paid by various professional groups of "royal men," as well as by the village of [al]*Na-nu-u*, which had to pay five sheqels.[78] Such forms of taxation suggest that the pasture-lands belonged not to the village-community but to the king.[79]

---

[76] "On" is preferable (cf. with *ʿl* in PRU, II, 10 above). It seems likely that this is the sum total which the *tamkars* had not yet delivered to the treasury. Therefore lines 15–19 could be scribal memory notes concerning *tamkars (mkrm)* who did not liquidate their obligations to the treasury.

[76a] About the role of the *tamkars* cf. *M. Heltzer*, *Tamkar* et son role dans l'Asie Occidentale de XIV–XIII siecles av. n.e., VDI, 1964, No. 2, pp. 3–16, (Russian), *A. F. Rainey*, Business agents in Ugarit, IEJ, XIII, 1963, pp. 313–21; *R. Yaron*, Foreign Merchants in Ugarit, ILR, IV, 1969, pp. 71–79; *M. Astour*, The Merchant Class of Ugarit, RAI, XVIII, München, 1972, pp. 11–26.

[77] PRU, III 16.153, where the [al]*E[. . .]iš* is freed from various duties and taxes and among them: 12) *u immêrātu*[M] *ma-aq-qa-du* ("and sheep, (pay for) pasture"). Cf. *Mendelsohn*, Samuel's Denunciation, p. 20.

[78] PRU, VI, 116 (RS. 17.64).

[79] *M. Heltzer*, On the Ownership of the Pastures in Ugarit, in "Studies in the History of the Jewish People and of the Land of Israel," III, Haifa, 1974, pp. 9–17 (Hebrew), p. III English summery.

Tithe paid in Grain

Tithes, paid to the king, made up a large part of the various taxes delivered in silver and agricultural products.[80] This was brilliantly demonstrated in the investigation of I. Mendelsohn.[81] The tithe is designated in the Akkadian texts from Ugarit as *ma-'a-ša-ru/ešrētu*.[82] There is no mention of a single individual paying the tithe. The tithe was imposed on the whole villiage as a collective body. We learn of one case in which the tithe consisted of grain *(šê)* and *šikāru* (the beer(?) made from barley).[83] The text PRU, III, 10.044 seems to record such tithes. According to this text, various villages of the kingdom of Ugarit paid grain, vine and oxen to the royal treasury.

Sometimes the tithe appeared under the name *miksu*, usually translated as "custom duty."[84] However, this translation is not exact. In the text PRU, III, 16.276 *miksu* appears in addition to the tithe *(ešrētu)* and other kinds of payments. This makes it possible to consider the term in a broader sense, sometimes covering various taxes, as well as custom-duties. From this we conclude, in agreement with F. R. Kraus, that *miksu* should be translated as "public payment from the field."[85]

But if we turn to the lists of payments of grain made by various villages of the kingdom of Ugarit, it is impossible to tell whether we are dealing with the tithe or not. Only the mention of grain as the tithe in PRU, III, 16.153[86] makes it possible to identify this form of taxation. Although the period of time for which the payment was due is not mentioned, we may assume that the lists refer to yearly payments.[87]

Table No. 2 classifies various data about the grain deliveries to the royal stores or treasury which Ugaritic villages *(âlu/qrit)* had to pay.

---

[80] *A. F. Rainey*, A Social Structure, pp. 96–108.

[81] *Mendelsohn*, Samuel's Denunciation, pp. 17–22.

[82] *Mendelsohn*, Samuel's Denunciation, p. 20. Cf. Hebr. *ma^caśēr* ("tithe"); mentioned in Ugarit in PRU, III, 16.153, ^{al}*E[. . .]iš;* 16.276, ^{al}*Uḫ-nap-pu;* 16.244, ^{al}*Bi-i-ru* had to pay; cf. also *M. A. Dandamajev*, Der Tempelzehnte in Babylonien während des 6.–4. Jh. v.u.Z. "Festschrift für Franz Altheim," Berlin, 1969, pp. 82–90; *E. Salonen*, Über den Zehnten im Alten Mesopotamien, Helsinki, 1972, pp. 60–61.

[83] PRU, III, 16.153, 10) *šê-šu šikar*^M*-šu* 11) *ša ma'a-ša-ri-šu* ("his grain and his *šikāru* of his tithe"), i.e. of the village *E[]iš*, when, in some cases, other products such as oil, cattle, etc., are mentioned without direct evidence, then we assume we are dealing with the tithe. Cf. also PRU, III, 16.269.

[84] Resp. ^{amel}*ma-ki-su* ("customer"); cf. PRU, IV, 17.134, 3–5, etc.

[85] *F. R. Kraus*, Ein Edikt des Königs Ammi-Ṣaduqa von Babylon, Leiden, 1958, pp. 141–42, "Öffentliche Feldabgabe."

[86] Cf. above, note 83.

[87] Cf. some texts which mention payments by some groups in Ugarit which had to be paid yearly: *ina šanāti*^M—PRU, III, 16.157, 21; 16.254D, 10; 15.132, 14, etc.

Table No. 2

No.	Village	Text	Amount of grain	Sort of grain	Delivery through[1]	Average from village
1.	[al]*A-ra-ni-ya*	PRU, III, 10.044	2 *kùr*	*ZÍ. KAL. MEŠ* "flour ?" "barley"	—	2 *kùr*
2.	[al]*U-bur-a*	,,	18 *kùr*	,,	—	18 *kùr*
3.	[al]*Bîru*	,,	[1]6 *kùr*	,,	—	[1]6 *kùr*
4.	[al]*Inu-qap-at*	,,	6 *kùr*	,,	—	} 6 *kùr*
	[al]*Inu-qa-pa[-at]*[2]	PRU, VI, 110 (RS. 19.88)	6 *kùr*[3]	,,	—	
5.	[al]*Be-ka-ni*	PRU, III, 10.044	50 *kùr*	,,	—	50 *kùr*
6.	[al]*Ili-iš-tam-'i*	,,	18 *kùr*	,,	—	18 *kùr*
7.	[al]*Šub-ba-ni*	,,	5 *kùr*	,,	—	5 *kùr*
8.	[al]*Ṭe$_4$-ba-qu*	,,	5 *kùr*	,,	—	} 8.5 *kùr*
	[al]*Ti-ba-qu*	PRU, VI, 106 (RS. 19.119)	12 *kùr*	—	—	
9.	[al]*Riq-di*	PRU, III, 10.044	18 *kùr*	*ZÍ. KAL. MEŠ*	—	18 *kùr*
10.	[al]*Šu-ra-šu*	,,	6 *kùr*	,,	—	6 *kùr*
11.	[al]*Iṣṣuru (ḪU)*	,,	6 *kùr*	,,	—	6 *kùr*
12.	[al]*Ib-na-li*	PRU, VI, 100 (RS. 19.51)	? *kùr*	—	—	—
13.	[al]*Pa-ša-ra-te*	PRU, VI, 102 (RS. 19.12)	40 *kùr*	*ZÍZ.AN.NA* (*kunašu* "emmer")	[1]*A-ri-ma-ri*	40 *kùr*
14.	[al]*Ma-ri-a-te*	,,	6 *kùr*	,,	[1]*Ši*[1]*-di-[n]a*	6 *kùr*
15.	[al]*Ia-a-pa-ru*	,,	40 *kùr*	,,	[1]*Zu-ga-u*	40 *kùr*
16.	[al]*Ia-a-lu*	,,	10 *kùr*	,,	[I]*Ši-ga-nu*	10 *kùr*

Table No. 2 continued

No.	Village	Text	Amount of grain	Sort of grain	Delivery through[1]	Average from village
17.	[al]*A-ru-tu*	PRU, VI, 102 (RS. 19.12)	—	”	—	6.25 *kùr*
		PRU, VI, 105 (RS. 19.117)	7 *kùr*	*šê* "grain"	*PA* (= *aklu* "overseer")	
		PRU, VI, 106 (RS. 19.119)	3 *kùr*	—	—	
		PRU, VI, 110 (RS. 19.88)	5(?) *kùr*	—	—	
		PRU, VI, 111 (RS. 19.129)	10 *kùr*	*šê* "grain"	—	
18.	[al]*Ša-lir$_x$-ba-a*	PRU, VI, 105 (RS. 19.117)	5 *kùr*	*šê* "grain"	*PA* (= *aklu*)	5 *kùr*
		PRU, VI, 111 (RS. 19.129)	5 *kùr*	*šê* "grain"	—	
19.	[al]*E-ku-na-mu* ug. *Yknᶜm)*	PRU, VI, 105 (RS. 19.117)	5 *kùr*	*šê* "grain"	*PA* (= *aklu*)	5 *kùr*
20.	[al]*Du-ma-tu*	PRU, VI, 105 (RS. 19.117)	5 *kùr*	*šê* "grain"	*PA* (= *aklu*)	5 *kùr*
		PRU, VI, 111 (RS. 19.129)	5 *kùr*	*šê* "grain"	—	
21.	[al]*A-ḫa-tu*	PRU, VI, 105 (RS. 19.117)	5 *kùr*	*šê* "grain"	*PA*	4 *kùr*
		PRU, VI, 111 (RS. 19.129)	3 *kùr*	”	—	
22.	[al]*Qa-ma-nu-zu*	PRU, VI, 105 (RS. 19.117)	5 *kùr*	*šê* "grain"	*PA*	5 *kùr*
23.	[al]*Ša-am-ra*	PRU, VI, 105 (RS. 19.117)	6 *kùr*	*šê* "grain"	—	6 *kùr*
		PRU, VI, 111 (RS. 19.129)	6 *kùr*	”	—	
24.	[al]*Qu-ur-tu*	PRU, VI, 105 (RS. 19.117)	?	*šê* "grain"	*PA*	?

No.	Village	Text	Amount of grain	Sort of grain	Delivery through[1]	Average from village
25.	^{al}*Ap-su-na*	PRU, VI,111 (RS. 19.129)	[x]	*šê* ”	—	?
26.	^{al}*Za-ri-nu*	PRU, VI,111 (RS. 19.129)	10 *kùr*	*šê* ”	—	10 *kùr*
27.	^{al}*Ša[m]-[na]* (?)	PRU,VI,111 (RS. 19.129)	6 *kùr*	*šê* "grain"	—	6 *kùr*
28.	^{al}*[Ša]l-ma-a* (?)	”	3 *kùr*	*šê*	—	3 *kùr*
29.	^{al}*Šu-wa-a*	”	x *kùr*	*šê*	—	x *kùr*
30.	^{al}*A-ga-nu*	CL. 1957,3	164 *kùr* 62 *kùr*	*šê MEŠ* *ZÍZ.AN NA. MEŠ* "emmer"	— *Iš-te-lu*	226 *kùr*
31.	*Ša'artu* (*SÍG, Š^{c}rt*)	”	52 *kùr* 53 *kùr*	*šê MEŠ* *ZÍZ.AN NA. MEŠ*	— —	105 *kùr*

[1] Tells to whom (*eli* x) the grain was given for preservation, storage or other purpose.

[2] ^{al}*Inu-qa-pa-[at]* instead of the reading of J. Nougayrol ^{al}*Ma[š?]-ka-na[. . .]*. The orthography shows that the first sign is by no means *maš* ▷┼, and that the only possible reading instead of *maš* is ▷— *ina* without the additional vertical stroke; cf. *W. von Soden, W. Röllig*, Das Akkadische Syllabar, Roma, 1967, No. 1. The third sign is the same *(PA)*, which recurs on tablets PRU, VI, 109 (RS. 19.191), 105 (19.117), etc.

[3] The figure seems more likely to be "6".

Table No. 2 records the grain payments made by thirty-one villages of Ugarit, but the specific amounts are known for only twenty-seven villages. Averages can be computed for seven villages from the data available. This data does not demonstrate any striking difference in payments from year to year, thus, it can be assumed that the amount recorded for the remaining villages is fairly accurate as an indicator of their average payments. The overall figures for the villages ranges from 2 *kùr* to 226 *kùr*. The total amount of grain for all twenty-seven villages is 635.75 *kùr*. (No distinction is made between barley and emmer.) The average for one village is 23.6 *kùr* of grain. From texts U.V. 143–52[88] we learn that the

[88] R. S. 20.10; 20.196; 20.161; 20.160; 20.14; 21.05; 21.65; 21.07; 21.196 A; RS 6 X; Rs. Pt. 1844.

kùr in Ugarit consisted of 300 *ka* (1.2 *ka* = 1 liter). Thus, 1 *kùr* was equivalent to approximately 250 liters.[89] As was demonstrated earlier, there were about 200 villages in Ugarit.[90] The treasury thus received approximately 4,700 *kùr* of grain (200×3.6 *kùr*)—a little less than 1200 metric tons.

The data also shows that, in some cases, the royal stores did not receive the grain tax directly from each village, but rather by delivery through certain individuals.[91] The text PRU, VI, 102 mentions four such persons: *Arimari*, *Šidina*, *Zuga'u* and *Šiganu*. Text Cl. 1957,3 mentions one such person, *Ištelu*. Instead of naming these individuals by name, PRU, VI, 105 designates them all with the Sumerian ideogram *PA* (*ugula*, Akk. *aklu*) "overseer." The above-mentioned names are given even without the fathers' names. Therefore there is no possibility to identify these overseers with Ugaritic officials known from other texts. But text PRU, VI, 105 seems to prove that all of them were *PA* "overseers." Perhaps their function was to control and oversee the regular payment of these taxes by the village-communities of Ugarit. It is interesting to note that in this case the taxes were not farmed by *tamkars (mkrm)* of the king of Ugarit, as was the case with the taxes paid in silver (cf. above pp. 33–34). We must remember that the amount of grain given here was received by the royal treasury of Ugarit only by payments from the rural communities and that it does not include the income of grain from the royal real estate which has been discussed in a separate work by this author.[92]

We know that in this same period the Hittite king purchased about 2,000 *kùr* of grain in the land of *Mukiš*. The task of transporting it by sea was imposed on the king of Ugarit who had to perform this task with his ships.[93] We can see that if 2,000 *kùr* was a considerable amount of grain for the Hittite kingdom then Ugarit was quite wealthy in this respect.

---

[89] About the ka in the contemporary Kassite Babylonia, cf. *B. Meissner*, Warenpreise in Babylon, Berlin, 1936, pp. 4–5.

[90] Cf. table No. 1 and accompanying comments.

[91] Cl, 1957, 3; PRU, VI, 102 and 105.

[92] *M. Heltzer*, "Royal Dependents"; the investigation does not include the editions of texts from U,V, PRU, VI and Claremont Tablets. The amount of grain, received from the landholdings of royal servicemen *(bnš mlk)* was a very little one.

[93] U,V, 33 (RS. 20.212), 19) [il]*Šamšu*[šu] *2 lim ŠE BAR[ ]* 20) *ul-tu* [mat]*Mu-kiš-ḫi uk-tal-lim-šu-nu-ti* ("The Sun (the Hittite king) assigned from the land of Mukiš 2000 *(kùr)* grain,") the order or transporting them by the ships of the king of Ugarit follows (lines 21–26), cf. the fragment U,V, 171 (RS. 26.158), cf. also *H. Klengel*, Geschichte Syriens, II, 395.

Some centuries later, in the middle of the tenth century b.c., king Solomon of Israel had to pay 20,000 *kùr* of wheat (grain)[94] yearly to Hiram, king of Tyre, for various types of timber which Solomon used for his building activities. If we compare this figure with the 5,000 *kùr* of grain received annually as tithes in Ugarit we see that, taking into account that the kingdom of Solomon was at least ten times larger than the kingdom of Ugarit, and that the income of Solomon must have been relatively the same, the figures are by no means exaggerated.

Payments of Wine

At least from the third millenium b.c. vineyards and wine production played a large economic role in Ugarit, as in most of the coastlands of the eastern Mediterranean. The mythological and epical literature of Ugarit is full of references to wine and its consumption. The ritual texts often explain that wine was used for offerings to the gods. One of the Ugaritic months was named *yrḫ rišyn*[95]/Akk. ^{arah}$_2$*rêš-karani*^{M}, "(month) of the head-of-the wine."[96] We also know about deliveris of large quantities of wine from the royal stores to be used for various purposes. So it is natural that a wine tax should have existed in Ugarit.

The wine tax was measured by jars *(kd/DUG/karpatu)*. Let us consider the tablet PRU, V, 4 (UT, 2004): 1) *yn. d. ykl. bd. [. . .] l. dbḥ mlk* 1) "The wine from (or "of the kind of") *ykl* for [. . .] 2) at the royal sacrifice."[97] The dividing line in the text is followed by a list of the gods of Ugarit together with the prescribed offerings for each of them.[98] The reverse of the tablet differs from all the other known texts of this type. It contains a list of the names of thirteen villages of the kingdom of Ugarit *(Lbnm, Ḫlb gngnt, Bṣr, Nnu, Šql, Šmny, Šmgy, Hzp, Bir, Agm, Šrš, Rqd, Uḫnp)* as well as

---

[94] I Reg 5,25 *ḥiṭṭīm* ("wheat") as well as ("grain") generally.

[95] *A. Herdner*, "Un nouvel exemplaire du rituel RS. 1929, No. 3," Syria, XXXIII, 1956, pp. 104–21 (UT, 173, 1), PRU, II, 106, 32 (UT, 1106), PRU, V, 12, 21 (UT, 2012); cf. *Gordon*, UT, p. 481, No. 2296.

[96] U, V, 99 (RS. 20.425), 13, date formula *i-na* ^{arah}$_2$*rêš-karāni*^{M}. Cf. also footnote of *J. Nougayrol*, P. 194, No. 3, RS. 19.25, 4, *ITU SAG GEŠTIN. MEŠ* = ^{arah}*rêš-karāni* in PRU, VI, 107, 11. On the Ugaritic months see, *J. P. J. Olivier*, Notes on the Ugaritic Month Names, JNSL, I, 1971, pp. 39–45; II, 1972, pp. 52–59; ***riš yn*** = Sept./Oct.

[97] Cf. *O. Eissfeldt*, Molk als Opferbegriff im Punischen und Hebräischen und das Ende des Gottes Moloch, Beiträge zur Religionsgeschichte des Altertums, 3, 1935. Cf. also *O. Eissfeldt*, Neue Keilalphabetische Texte aus Ras Schamra-Ugarit, Berlin, 1965, p. 14.

[98] *A. Herdner*, Un nouvelle, PRU, II, 4 and 5 (UT, 1004–5), etc.

the number of "jars of wine" *(kd yn)* which they had to deliver. Every village was required to deliver from 2–10 jars. Thus, we have here a special wine tax for sacrificial purposes. It may have been connected with the temple economy.

Another text, CTC, 67 (UT, 110), records the total sum of "148 jars of wine totally" (13) *1 me-at 48 DUG GEŠTIN napḫar*). This text, as well as PRU, III, 10.044, discussed above in connection with the grain tax and confirming the yearly character of the payments, helps us somewhat in reconstructing this tax. Table No. 3 summarizes the information found in these two texts concerning wine payments.

Table No. 3 shows a total of 160 jars of wine from fourteen villages, i.e. an average of 11.5 jars pers village. The total for the estimated 200 villages of Ugarit would thus be approximately 2,300 jars of wine. But source documents are so scarse at the present time that we cannot draw definitive conclusions.

Table No. 3

No.	Village	Quantity	Measuring Unit	Text No.
1.	*Ḫlb ^{c}prm*	*ṯṯ* (6)	*DUG*	CTC, 67 (UT, 110)
2.	*Ḫlb krd*	*ṯn ^{c}šr* (12)	"	" " " "
3.	*Qmy*	*arb^{c} ^{c}šr* (14)	"	" " " "
4.	*Ṣ^{c}q*	*arb^{c} ^{c}šr* (14)	"	" " " "
5.	*Ṣ^{c}*	*ṯmn* (8)	"	" " " "
6.	*Šḥq*	*^{c}šrm arb^{c}* (24)	"	" " " "
7.	*Ḫlb rpš*	*arb^{c} ^{c}šr* (14)	"	" " " "
8.	*Bq^{c}t*	*ṯṯ* (6)	"	" " " "
9.	*Irab*	*ṯn ^{c}šr* (12)	"	" " " "
10.	*Ḥbš*	*ṯmn* (8)	"	" " " "
11.	*Amḏy*	*arb^{c} ^{c}šr* (14)	"	" " " "
12.	*[G]n^{c}y*	*ṯṯ* (6)	"	" " " "
13.	^{al}*Šu-ra-šu*	11	*DUG. GEŠTIN*	PRU, III, 10.044, 12[1]
14.	^{al}*Iṣṣuru (ḪU)*	17	"	PRU, III, 10.044, 13[2]

[1] *Šrš* (^{al}*Šu-ra-šu*) appears also in PRU, V, 4, 32 where the village has to deliver 7 jars of wine.

[2] Lines 14–15 of the same text tell about 12 and 7 jars of wine respectively, but the names of the villages are not preserved on the tablet.

It should be noted that, as in all the previously discussed cases, each village is treated as a single unit.

Payments in Olive Oil

From various Ugaritic texts, especially from tablets containing legal documents concerning land transactions, we know of the important role played by olive trees *(ᶦˢserdu*ᴹᴱŠ*)* in the economy of Ugarit. The royal *gt (dimtu)* served as centers where olive oil from the royal estates, taxes, and other income, was produced and stored.[99] Since olive oil was so important in the economy, it is only natural that a tax on this commodity was exacted. Oil *([šam]nu)* is mentioned as the tax from the *âlu Beqa-ᶦˡIštar.*[100] Tax lists which would indicate the number of *âlu/qrit* having to pay taxes in olive oil are currently unavailable. However, PRU, II, 82 (UT, 1082) seems to be a completely preserved list of all, or almost all, the households of a whole village from whom the olive oil tax was collected. The first line reads: 1) *kd. šmn. ᶜl Hbm Šlm[y]* ("(One) jar of oil on (i.e. for derlivery)[101] *Hbm, man of Šlmy.*"). Lines 2–26 and Rev. 1–7 list the names of thirty-two persons; only three lines are reconstructed. Every line begins with x (the number) *kd(m) ᶜl y* ("x jar(s) on (for delivery by) y"). At least eighteen persons (including *Hbm*) had to deliver 1 jar of olive oil; 3 persons had to deliver 2 jars; 2 persons had to deliver 3 jars; 2 persons had to deliver 4 jars. For the other persons the numbers in the text are not legible. At the end of the text the total figure is given as Rev. 8) *tgrm. šmn. d bn. Kwy* 9) *ᶜl. Šlmym. ṯmn. kbd* 10) *ṯṯm šmn* ("8) Totally[102] oil from *bn Kwy* 9) on (for delivery by) the people of *Šlmy* in all 10) 68 (jars of) oil"). Thus we see that the village *Šlmy* had to pay, perhaps annually, a tax of 68 jars of olive oil. The tax, as in other cases in which taxes were distributed among the households of the villagers, was not distributed equally. *Bn Kwy* could be an individual responsible for collecting the tax, similar to the *tamkars* mentioned in PRU, V, 107 or to the "overseers" responsible for collecting the grain tax.

---

[99] *Heltzer*, "Royal Dependents," pp. 40–47; *Heltzer*, Problems, pp. 42–43.
[100] PRU, III, 16.269, 18.
[101] Cf. above, text PRU, V, 107, note No. 76.
[102] Scribal error, *tgrm* instead of *tgmr* ("total(ly)").

Taxes Paid in Cattle

Apart from the mixed tax paid in silver and cattle there was a tax paid only in cattle (cf. above p. 34). PRU, III, 10.044, mentioned above in connection with grain and wine taxes, also refers to oxen *(GUD-alpu)* paid to the royal treasury. This seems to be, as in other cases, an annual payment. [al]*Šu-ra-šu*, [al]*Iṣṣuru (ḪU)*, and [al]*A-ra-ni-ya*, together with another *âlu* whose name was in the broken part of the tablet, had to deliver 1 ox from 2 villages. [al]*U-bur-a*, [al]*Bêru*, and four other villages whose names are completely illegible (lines 14–17) had to deliver one each. The same obligation may have been demanded of [al]*Riqdi(?)* (line 11). [al]*Be-qa-ni* was obliged to deliver 13 oxen. Text PRU, V, 39 (UT, 2039), 17 also mentions *Tbq alp*, "the village *Tbq*—(one) ox," in addition to the taxes paid in sheep from the village *Ṯlṯ* (cf. below).

PRU, V, 64 (UT, 2064) deserves special attention. This text comes from the tablet-baking furnace. It is a letter of a royal official.[103] The first part, which is badly preserved, consists of greetings. The text goes on to relate that "the king gives pretty horses to *ᶜbdyrḫ* (16) *w. ml[k]. $s_2s_2$wm nᶜmm* 17) *ytn. lᶜbdyrḫ*), and adds: "And according to the tablets, ploughing oxen, on your demand from me, the people of *Bly* have chosen. The oxen (are) for you and for me" (21) *w. lḥt. alpm. ḥrṯm* 22) *k. rgmt. ly Blym* 23) *alpm. aršt. lk. w. ly*).[104] So we see that the people of *Bly*, which was an Ugaritic village, had to deliver ploughing oxen for the royal estates. However, in this case the king made a concession and handed some of the oxen over to the author of the message contained in PRU, V, 64, perhaps for use by the latter in his household.

PRU, V, 39 (UT, 2039) gives information about the sheep tax. The tablet has the heading 1) *b Ṯlṯ* ("in (the village) *Ṯlṯ*").[105] Then the text lists 2) *[I]lmlk. ᶜšr ṣin* 3) *Mlknᶜm ᶜšr.* 4) *bn. Adty ᶜšr* 5) *[Ṣ]dqšlm ḫmš* 6) *Krzn. ḫmš* 7) *Ubrᶜym ḫmš* ("2) *[I]lmlk*—10 small cattle 3) *Mlknᶜm*—10 4) *bn Adty*—10 5) *[Ṣ]dqšlm*—5 6) *Krzn*—5 7) people of *Ubrᶜy*—5"). The

---

[103] A partial analysis of the text is found in *M. Heltzer*, VDI, 1966, No. 3, pp. 201–202 (Russian).

[104] *'rš*—cf. UT, p. 367, No. 379, "to request." On the interpretation "to chose" see, *M. Heltzer, A Charsekin*, New Inscriptions from Pirgi in Etruscan and Phoenician, VDI, 1965, No. 3, pp. 111–12 (Russian). The term *lḥ* ("tablet")—UT, p. 427, No. 1358.

[105] In disagreement with *Ch. Virolleaud* (PRU, V, p. 53), who translates "for three (sheqels of silver)." We know the village *Ṯlṯ*/[al]*Su-la-du*/*S_2ld*/*Ṯlṯ* well; cf. table No. 1, 134. This place-name appears in PRU, IV, 17.340, v.7; 17.62; PRU, V, 41 (UT, 2041); PRU, VI, 118 (RS. 18.116), 2.

following lines (8–16) list 9 persons whose names are only partly legible. Each was obliged to deliver only one small animal. It is not clear to which village these people belonged. As was pointed out above (p. 43) the village *Tbq* had to deliver one ox *(alp)*. It seems that the persons named in the tablet were head of families. A significant feature of this text is its revelation of the way in which the tax was divided amount the members of the community. This was not done on the basis of full equality between the families. The text, which mentions only certain villages, probably does not list all the families of the community. It is possible that some families in the community did not have to pay every tax. However, the scarsity of information at the present time prevents us from drawing definitive conclusions.

Only one tablet (CL. 1957.4) records a large number of sheep paid by one single village, 1) 68 *UDU. NIN. MA* 2) ^{I}*Ili-ya-na mâr Ba-ri-ya* 3) ^{al}*Ili-iš-tam-i* ("1) 68 spring lambs 2) (through) *Iliyana*, son of *Bariya* 3) (from) *Ilištam'i*."). Although the text is very brief, we see that the tax was delivered through a certain person, perhaps an *aklu*, "overseer." As noted before, this was the case in regard to the grain tax. A particularly interesting aspect of the tax is the fact that the village had to pay "spring lambs," probably a part of the yearly natural increase of the villagers' flocks. The lack of more detailed information prevents us from drawing further conclusions.

Taxes Paid in Artifacts

Information about taxes paid in utensils is found in the tablet PRU, III, 15.20. According to this source at least 4 *âlu* (^{al}*Aš(?)-pu*, ^{al}*Gul-ba-ta*, ^{al}*Ya-al-du*, ^{al}*U-bu-zu)* had to deliver two bronze vessels each. It is not clear who produced these bronze vessels *(TAL. MEŠ. siparri)*.

Text PRU, VI, 134 (RS. 19. 19A) records the delivery of lances *(šennū*^{M}*)* from various villages of the kingdom to the royal stores. The text reads as follows:[105a]

1) $^{\mathrm{[a]l}}$*A-ru-tu 30 šen[nū*^{M} *i-bi-la]*	*Arutu* [brought (delivered)] 30 lan[ces]
2) *5 šennū ir-te-ḫa*	5 lances ? remained (for delivery)
3) ^{al}*Ša-li-ma-a 12 šennū*^{M} *i-bi-l[a]*	*Šalima* delivered 12 lances
4) *8 šennū*^{M} *ir-te-ḫa*	8 lances ? remained (for delivery)

105a On this text cf. *A. F. Rainey*, IOS, III, 1973, p. 47; *C. Kühne*, UF, V, 1973, p. 189.

5) ^{al}*Ya-ku-naᶜamu 15 šennū i-bi-la* 6) *10 šennū*^{M} *ir-te-ḫa*	*Yakunaᶜamu* delivered 15 lances 10 lances ? remained
7) ^{al}*Šá-lir*$_{\mathrm{x}}$*-ba 16 šennū*^{M} *i-bi-la* 8) *6 šennū*^{M} *ir-te-ḫu*	*Šalirba* delivered 15 lances 6 lances ? remained
9) ^{al}*[Qa]-ra-tu 35 še[nn]ū [i-bi-la]*[106] 10) *[š]a-lim*	*[Qa]ratu* [delivered] 35 l[anc]es ? fully!
11) *[*^{al}*Za]-ri-nu 29 š[ennū*^{M}*]* 12) *[x šenn]ū ir-te-ḫa*	*[Za]rinu* (delivered) 29 la[nces] ? [x lance]s ? remained
13) [^{al}]*Ap-su-na 40 šennū*^{M} *ša-[lim]* 14) [^{a}]^{l}*Šam-ra-a*[107] *15 šennū*^{M}	*Apsuna* 40 lances ? fully! *Šamra* (delivered) 15 lances ?
15) *[x šennū] ir-te-[ḫ]a* 16) *[*^{al}*A-ḫ]a-tu [x+] 1 šennū*^{M}	[x lances] ? rema[in]ed (for delivery) *[Aḫ]atu* (delivered) $x+1$ lances ?
17) *[x šennū] ir-te-[ḫ]u*	[x lances] ? remai[ne]d (for delivery)
18) *[ ] ??? [ ]*[108]	

It is difficult to say how and by whom these arms were produced. Until now the only information we have indicates that these were produced by royal artisans.[109] It is possible that the villagers, or villages as a whole, had to buy the required artifacts from the royal artisans. But is seems more likely that the villagers produced the arms themselves and had to deliver them to the royal stores as tax payments. In this frame work this nine villages had to deliver lances. The number which every village had to deliver varies. Only *Qaratu* and *Apsuna* fulfilled the whole obligation. The rest of the *âlu/qrit* remained debtors and were obliged to fulfill the obligation in the near future. Here again the village is treated as a single unit with no indication of how payment of the tax was distributed among the households or individual families. About 20–40 spears (lances) were demanded from each village.

---

[106] Our reconstruction. In all other cases, unless otherwise specified, reconstruction of the text is by *J. Nougayrol*.

[107] *Šam-ra-a*, read by *J. Nougayrol U-ra-a; Ura* is known as a city in Asia Minor. The sign can be read also as *šam*, and this is preferable.

[108] It seems that the last broken line gave the total figure of lances (?) delivered and still to be delivered; cf. *Rainey* and *Kühne*, "kettles" instead of "lances" since the ideogram *ŠEN. MEŠ* usually means "kettles," and the translation of *J. Nougayrol* (PRU, VI, 155, No. 5) is based on an unpublished text.

[109] *M. Heltzer*, Organizatsiya remeslennovo proizvodstva v Ugarite, PS, XIII, 1965, p. 47ff. (Hebrew translation, *'rgwn hml'kh b'wgryt* in *Ml'kh, ṣb' wnwhg mšpṭy b'wgryt, Yršlym, tšl'* (1970) pp. 1–25.)

One form of the labor tax, according to the available information involved the distribution to the villages of raw materials, from which certain artifacts were to be produced. These artifacts were to be turned over to the royal treasury, as shown in the text given above. According to text PRU, VI, 113 (RS. 19.26) the villages received raw materials for the production of certain wooden objects.

1) *2 ME 20*^{iṣM}	220 (trunks) of
2) *ma-á[s-w]a-tu*	of *ma[sw]atu*—timber[110]
3) *a-na a[mêlē]*^{M} ^{al}*A-r[u]tu*	for the peo[ple] of (the village) *Arutu*
4) *2 ME 3[0](?)* ^{iṣM}	230(?) tree trunks
5) *ma-sa-wa-tu-[m]a*	of *maswatu*—timber
6) *a-na* ^{al}*Ib-na-li-ya*	for (the people) of (the village) *Ibnaliya*

We see that the people of *Arutu* and *Ibnaliya*, each mentioned as a single body, received quantities of timber to be used in some type of sort. It should be noted that *Arutu* appears in the text PRU, VI, 134 (RS. 19.19A) among the villages delivering lances ? Thus it is very possible that the text under discussion is describing the delivery of raw materials not to professionals, i.e. royal dependents, but to villagers. The latter, in this view, had to produce artifacts from the raw materials and to turn over these artifacts to the royal treasury as taxes.

Various Unidentified Taxes and Duties

PRU, V, 78 (UT, 2078), one of the tablets from the tablet-baking furnace, which was quoted above (p. 23), talks about 1) *Rišym qnum*, "People of (the village) *Riš qnum* (pl.)."[111] It appears that in this quote we are dealing with a participle of the root **qn'*, and that the word designates a certain action which the people had to perform. The text lists, by their names and the names of their fathers, 21 persons who had to perform this obligation.

---

[110] Meaning unknown, but apparently not a precious type of timber; cf. AHW, p. 619 and *Rainey*, IOS, III, p. 46.

[111] The word cannot be convincingly interpreted. *Ch. Virolleaud*, PRU, V, p. 104, translates it as "purple dyers"; *C. H. Gordon*, UT, p. 479, No. 2246, translates it as "to be zealous," but this is also unacceptable.

It seems likely that PRU, V, 75 (UT, 2075), also from the tablet-baking furnace, belongs to the group of duty or corvée texts. The heading 1) *spr rpš d l y[dy]*,[112] "List of *rpš(?)* which are at *ydy(?)*."[113] Lines 2–5 list 4 villages; the personal name *bn Sḫrn* follows in line 6. Lines 6–12 list 6 names of villages followed by 7 personal names in lines 13–19. The reverse (line 20) begins again with *rpš d. ydy* and following 8 village names (lines 21–28) *bn Ḥgby* (line 29) is named. The text is concluded by the name of the village *Mrat* (line 30). Perhaps at the end of the existence of the kingdom of Ugarit some large families grew into small villages, which were designated by the name of the founding family. This development could explain why family names are mixed together with village names in this text. However, no conclusive evidence is presently available. Other fragmentary texts which are available mayby be concerned with taxes and duties. However, at the present time no definitive interpretation is possible.[114]

Conclusions

The above discussion has outlined the duties, taxes and other obligations of the villages of Ugarit insofar as these are determinable from currently available sources. The most important conclusions emerging from our analyses are: 1) Villages, as collective units, were obligated to meet all taxes and duties placed upon them by the royal government. This demonstrates the communal character of the Ugaritic village, which should thus be considered a rural community. 2) Within the rural community the taxes, labor obligations, and so on, with the possible exception of military conscription, were not necessarity distributed equally among all the villagers. The tax burdens may have been distributed on the basis of the amount of property owned, or on the basis of family size.

---

[112] The reconstruction of *Ch. Virolleaud*, PRU, V, p. 104, *y[dym(?)]* is without any real foundation.

[113] Cf. line 20 of the same text—*rpš. d ydy*.

[114] PRU, III, 11.800; 15.183; 15.189; 15.179; PRU, V, 17 (UT, 2017). 1) *Miḫdym*, "People of (the village) *Miḫd*," followed by eight personal names; 21 (UT, 2021) 1) *[s]p[r] Ušknym. dt. b[d?]*, "List of people of (the village) *Uškn* who [ ]," at least thirty personal names follow; 22 (UT, 2022); 24 (UT, 2024); 25 (UT, 2025); 41 (UT, 2041) village names; 74 (UT, 2074) village names; 77 (UT, 2077) village names; 118 (UT, 2118); 144; 145; 146; 147; 165; U, V, 102 (RS. 20.207A); 103 (RS. 20.143B); 104 (RS. 20.144); PRU, VI, 94 (RS. 17.431); 96 (RS. 19.91); 97 (RS. 19.118); 169 (RS. 18.279), etc.

CHAPTER III

ROYAL GRANTS OF TAX AND LABOR OBLIGATIONS TO HIGH FUNCTIONARIES

We possess a number of legal texts from Ugarit, written in Akkadian, concerning grants of the obligations of certain villages to certain individuals. Full texts and excerpts from these texts follow.

1. PRU, III, 16.276.

1) *iš-tu ûmi an-ni-im* 2) ^{I}*Niq-ma-*^{il}*Adu mâr Am-mi-[is-tam-]ri* 3) *šàr* ^{al}*Ú-ga-ri-it* 4) *it-ta-din* ^{al}*Úḫ-nap-p[i]* 5) *a-na* ^{I}*KAR-*^{il}*Kušuḫ mâr A-na-a[n] u a-na* ^{f}*A-pa-pa-a* 7) *mârat šarri*^{ri} 8) *qa-du ešrēti[?]-ša qa-du* 9) *miksi-ša qa-du* 10) *ši-ir-ki-ša ma-am-ma* 11) *a-na* ^{al}*Uḫ-nap-pi*^{ki} 12) *la-a i-ra-gu-um* 13) *a-na* ^{I}*KAR-*^{il}*Kušuḫ u* 14) *a-na* ^{f}*A-pa-pa-a u* 15) *a-na mâri*^{M} ^{f}*A-pa-pa-a* 16) ^{al}*Uḫ-nap-pi*^{ki} *id[-din](?)* 17) *ša-ni-tam* ^{I}*KAR-*^{il}*Kušuḫ* 18) *za-ki ki-ma* ^{il}*Šamši*^{ši} 19) *a-na da-ri-it-ti* 20) *ar-ka-na-šu za-k[i]* 21) *bîtum*^{tum} ^{il}*Ba*c*al ḫuršan [Ḫa-zi]* 22) *u* ^{amelM}*ku-um-[ra-šu](?)* 23) ^{I}*KAR-*^{il}*Kušuḫ* 24) *la-a u-te-bu-u.*

"1) From the present day: 2) *Niqmaddu*, son of *Ammi[stam]ru*, 3) king of Ugarit 4) gave (the village) *Uḫnappu* 5) to *Kar-Kušuḫ*, son of *Ana[n]u* 6) and (to) *Apapa*, 7) daughter of the king, 8) together with the tithe, 9) together with its taxes[1] together 10) with its offerings. Nobody 11) shall have any claims 12) (concerning) *Uḫnappu.* 13) To *Kar-Kušuḫ* and 14) to *Apapa* and 15) to the sons of *Apapa* 16) (the village) *Uḫnappu* he ga[ve]. 17) Further: *Kar-Kušuḫ* 18) is pure like[2] the Sun, 19) forever. 20) For the length (of his life) he is pure.[3] 21) The house (sanctuary) of Baal of Mount *[Ḫazi]*[4] 22) and its prie[sts] ? 23) (to) *Kar-Kušuḫ* 24) may have no claims."

From this text it is clear that the royal princess, the daughter of the king, and her husband, received the right to demand and collect for themselves the taxes and labor obligations of the village *Uḫnappu.* We may thus assume that this was not a long-term grant. Perhaps it was only valid for the lifetime of the recipients. The text also seems to indicate that

---

[1] *miksu*, cf. above, Ch. II, p. 35.

[2] Typical formula used in freeing one of various obligations in Ugarit.

[3] First comes the standard expression of freedom from obligations forever, followed by the more exact definition that the freedom from obligations is only for the lifetime of the individual.

[4] Mount *Ṣafōn*, classical *Mons Casius*, modern Djebel-el Aqra, cf. *W. F. Albright*, Baal-Żephon, "Festschrift für *A. Bertholet*," Tübingen, 1950, p. 4ff.

before this gift was made the sanctuary of *Baal-Ṣafon* had some special privileges in the village of *Uḫnappu.*

2. PRU, III, 16.269.

This text relates that a certain *Gabanu* killed "*Yatarmu,* the scribe" (7) *Ya-tar-mu* ^{amel}*tupšarrum*^{rum}), "for he was an enemy . . . of the king his lord" (7) *i-nu-ma na-kir* . . . 8) *it-ti šarri bêli-šu*). The text continues to relate that *Gabanu* "gives (the village) *Be-qa-*^{il}*Ištar* to the king according to the law" (9) . . . *i-na-din* 10) ^{al}*Be-qa-*^{il}*Ištar a-na šarri* 11) *aš-šum dîni-šu-ma*). It seems that *Yatarmu* formerly possessed this village, or its obligations and taxes. The text continues: "11) . . . his lord 12) gave as a gift 13) to *Gabbanu* and his sons (it)." (11) . . . *bêli-šu* 12) *na-din ni-id-nu-uš* 13) *a-na* ^{I}*Gáb-ba-na a-na mâri*^{M}*-šu*). It is very probably that the text is referring to the same village *Beqa-Ištar*. After that the tablet mentions which taxes and obligations *Gabbanu* is no longer obligated to pay to the king. Although the text is broken we can read: 18) "[his grain, oi]l (and) beer 19) his [oxen] (and) sheep." The rest of the text is broken. It may be that these taxes also came from *Beqa-Ištar,* but because of the break in the tablet this is not definitively clear.

3. PRU, III, 16.244.

1) *iš-tu*^{I} $_{2}$*ûmi an-ni-i-im* 2) ^{I}*N[iq-m]e-pa mâr Niq-ma-*^{il}*Addu* 3) *šàr Ú-ga-ri-it* 4) *it-ta-ši kasap*^{M} ^{amelM}*šar-ra-ku-ti* 5) *ù kasap* ^{amelM}*zi-in-ḫa na-še* 6) *ù kasap* ^{amelM}*ti-pa-li na-še* 7) *ù ma-ša-ra ša* ^{al}*Bêri* 8) *ù it-ta-din-šu* 9) *a-na* ^{I}*En-ta-ša-li* 10) ^{amel}*Sākini* ^{al}*Bêri* 11) *a-na ûme*^{M} $_{2}$*balaṭi gamrūti*^{M} 12) ^{I}*En-ta-ša-li* 13) *ma-am-ma la-a i-la-qi-šu* 14) *iš-tu qa-ti-šu.*

"1) From this day 2) *Ni[qm]epa,* son of *Niqmaddu,* 3) king of Ugarit, 4) withdrew the silver of the offerers 5) and the silver of the . . .[5] people, 6) and the silver of the . . . people[6] 7) and the tithe of (the village) *Bêru* 8) and gave it 9) *to Entašalu,* 10) the *sākinu*[7] of *Bêru* 11) for the lifetime 12) of *Entašalu.* 13) Nobody shall take (it away) 14) from his hands."

This text clearly relates that only the taxes and other payments, not the village itself, was handed over to a certain high official.

4. PRU, III, 15.114.

1) *[i]š-tu ûmi*^{mi} *[annim]* 2) ^{I}*A-mis-tam-ru mâr Niq-me-p[a]* 3) *sàr* ^{al}*Ú-ga-ri-i[t]* 4) *it-ta-ši eqlāt*^{M} ^{I}*Ta-ri-[ ]* 5) *ù eqlāt*^{M} *Ku-ḫi-ia-na âli* 6) *ù* ^{al}*At-ka-šak-na u it-t[a-din-šu]* 7) *a-na Ták-ḫu-li-na* ^{amel}*sākin*[7] *ekallim*

[5] Meaning unclear. *J. Nougayrol,* PRU, III, p. 93, "portes d'ordures," i.e. a certain fine for scolding ?!; CAD, v. 16, p. 20, *ṣinḫu,* "excrement."

[6] *J. Nougayrol,* PRU, III, p. 93, "contraventions," "deliquencies(?)."

[7] *MAŠKIM.* On the reading of this ideogramm in the Akkadian texts from Ugarit, cf. table No. 1, note No. 46. The *sākinu* of the village was certainly the representative of the royal authorities; *E. Lipinski,* UF, V, 1973, pp. 106–97.

8) *ù -Ták-ḫu-li-nu* 9) *ᵃˡŠa-ak-na i-ra-ṣa-ap* 10) *i-na kaspiᴹ-šu i-na êriᴹ-šu* 11) *i-na gab-bi mim-mi-šu* 12) *u šarru ú-za-ki* 13) *ᵃˡŠa-a[k]-na i-na píl-ki* 14) *alpuᴹ-š[u-nu im]êrūᴹ-šu-nu* 15) *amêluᴹ[-šu-nu]* 16) *i-na š[i-ip-ri] šarriʳⁱ* 17) *[. . . la(?) il-l]a-ku.* (The rest of the tablet is broken.)

"1 [F]rom [this] day 2) *Ammistamru*, son of *Niqmep[a]*, 3) king of Ugari[t] 4) withdrew the fields of *Tari[x]* 5) and the fields of *Kuḫiana* of the village (town ?) 6) and (the village) *Atka-Šakna* and ga[ve it] 7) to *Takḫulinu*, the *sākinu* (vizier) of the palace. 8) And *Takḫulinu* 9) shall reconstruct (the village) *Šakna* 10) for his silver and copper 11) (and) on his (own) full expense. 12) And the king freed 13) (the village) *Šakna* from the obligation. 14) Its oxe[n], [its don]keys 15) [its] people 16) to the royal w[ork] 17) [. . . must not] go."

Here we see that the king handed over a complete village to a high official —*Takḫulinu*—who was the majordomo *(sākin ekallim)*.[8] *Takḫulinu* had to rebuild the village at his own expense. The village was freed from taxes and duties to the king. These were handed over to *Takḫulinu*, at least for a certain period.

5. PRU, III, 15.147.

This text consists of some royal gifts given by the king *Ammistamru II*. We read there:

V° 5') . . . *a-nu-um-ma* 6') *ᵃˡWa-na-a-lum rêš qa-du [eqli?-šu]* 7') *ù ᵃˡŠa-pí-ìl qa-du e[qli(?)-šu(?)]* 8') *it-ta-din-šu-nu šarru* 9') *a-na ᴵA-mu-ta-ru-na* 10') *ù a-na mârēᴹ-šu a-di da-[ri-ti]* 11') *ù ᴵA-mu-ta-ru-nu* 12') *u-ra-ṣi-ip-šu-nu* 13') *ù ú-še-ši-ib-šu-nu* 14') *amêlu ma-am-ma-an* 15') *la-a i-la-aq-qi-šu-nu* 16') *iš-tu qâti ᴵA-mu-ta-ru-ra* 17') *u iš-tu qâti mârēᴹ-šu a-di da-ri-[ti]*

"5') . . . So 6') (the village) *Wanalum*-the-High 7') and the low together with [its] fi[elds] 8') the king (*Ammistamru* II) gave 9') to *Amutarunu* 10') and his sons forev[er]. 11') And *Amutarunu* 12') shall rebuild them 13') and populate them. 14') Nobody 15') shall take them 16') from *Amutarunu* 17') and his sons foreve[r]."

The purpose of the grant is to repopulate and to rebuild a village devastated by war, disease, etc. It seems that *Amutarunu* received in return the right to collect all taxes and duties for himself. The text thus deals with the recreation of a village. But the principle on which the community was established is not specifically mentioned.

6. PRU, III, 16.153.

1) *i[š-t]u ûmiᵐⁱ an-ni-i-im* 2) *ᴵA[m-mi-]is-ta-a[m]-r[u mâ]r Niq-me-pa* 3) *šàr ᵃ⁽ˡ⁾Ú-ga-r[i-i]t* 4) *ᵃˡE[XX]iš qa-du₄* 5) *ga-ab-bi m[i]im-mi šum-ši-ša*

[8] Cf. *skn. bt. mlk*—PRU, II, 7 (UT, 1007), 5–6; cf. also *M. Heltzer*, Royal Ad-

6) *id-din a-na* ^I^*Ya-ṣi-ra-na* 7) *mâr* ^I^*Ḫu-ṣa-na* 8) *a-na da-ri-iš* 9) *a-na mârē*^M^ *mârē*^M^*-šu* 10) *šê*^M^*-šu šikar*^M^*-šu* 11) *ša ma-'a-ša-ri-ša* 12) *ù immerātu*^M^; *ma-aq-qa-du* 13) *a-na* ^I^*Ya-ṣi-ra-ma(!)* 14) *kasap ša-ra-ku-ti* 15) *ù kasap sú-sà-pí-in-nu-ti* 16) *a-na* ^I^*Ya-ṣi-ra-ma(!)*

"1) F[ro]m this day 2) *A[mmi]sta[m]r[u,* so]n of *Niqmepa,* 3) king of Ugar[i]t 4) gave (the village) *E[xx]-iš* 5) together with all that it 6) has, to *Yaṣiranu* 7) son of *Ḫuṣanu* 8) forever 9) (and) to his sons (and) grandsons. 10) Its grain (and) its beer 11) of the tithe,[9] 12) and the sheep: pasturing (tax)[10] 13) to *Yaṣiranu* (he gave). 14) The silver of the offerings (or offerers),[11] 15) and the silver of the bestmen[12] 16) (he gave) to *Yaṣiranu.*"

Once again we have a more or less complete description of the taxes and duties handed over by the king to *Yaṣiranu*, possibly for his merits or services. But this text declares clearly that *Yaṣiranu* received the right to collect the tithe and pasture-tax as well as two taxes (silver of the offerings (or offerers) and silver of the bestmen) which seemed to be irregular and occassional.

7. PRU, III, 16.202.

This tablet relates only that king *Ammistamru II* delivered the village *Kumba* (^al^*Ku-um-ba)* to a certain *Tulaya* and his sons. No other details are given.

The documents presented above show us that: a) the village was treated as a single unit—a community; b) the recipient of the village did not receive any right of ownership over the lands and people of the village. He received only the right to collect for himself the regular and irregular taxes and duties. It also seems likely that despite the fact that some texts stated that the granting of a village applied to the children and grandchildren of the favoured individual, the endowment was really for a shorter period, possibly the lifetime of the recipient. None of the available texts mention military conscription and it may be assumed that this right remained in the hands of the king. All in all there is not enough available information to make any comparison with the European feudalism of the middle ages as has been proposed by some scholars.[13]

---

ministration and Palace Personnel in Ugarit (Russian), LAMMD, X, 1969, pp. 227–28; *M. Dietrich, O. Loretz, J. Sanmartín*, UF, VI, 1974, pp. 41–42, No. 15.

[9] Cf. above, Ch. II, p. 35–40.

[10] Cf. above, Ch. II, p. 34.

[11] Cf. above, p. 31; PRU, III, 16.244.

[12] *Nougayrol*, PRU, III, p. 147, "garçons d'honneur"; cf. AHW, p. 1063, "Brautführer"—"bestman," "bridgeroom's supporter."

[13] *Rainey*, Social Structure, pp. 31–36 (including the previous bibliography); *A. F. Rainey*, The Kingdom of Ugarit, BA, XXVIII, 1965, No. 4, pp. 102–25.

CHAPTER IV

NON-PERFORMANCE OF OBLIGATIONS BY THE VILLAGERS AND THEIR DEFECTION FROM UGARIT

The *nayyālu*

Even though the whole community bore collective responsibility for fulfillment of tax and other obligations, all taxes and duties were distributed among the individual families inside the community. The sources present us with an opportunity to learn the reaction of individuals who could not fulfill their obligations as well as the treatment of these individuals by the authorities.

The nayyālu. This term is known not only from Ugarit, but only in texts from Ugarit (and some rare Middle Assyrian legal texts) is it used to mean "the man who did not perform his obligations."[1] The term itself seems to be a derivate from the word *niālu (nīʾlu)*—*nayyālu*—verbal adjective, nomen actionis from the D-stem of *nīlu*, meaning "idler," "lazy."

There are instances in the sources of royal servicemen being mentioned among the *nayyālu*. These individuals were deprived of their landholdings. The texts also deal with members of the rural communities who defaulted on their obligations and had their land taken by the authorities. The confiscated land was handed over to other persons. The texts which can be interpreted as concerning the members of the rural communities are given below.

1. PRU, III, 16.248.

1) *iš-tu* $_2$*ûmi an-ni-im* 2) ^{I}*Niq-ma-*^{il}*Addu mâr Am-m[i-is-tam-ri]* 3) *it-ta-ši bît-šu eqil*^{M}*-šu* 4) *gáb-bá mi-im-mi-šu ša* ^{I}*Ig-ma-ra-*^{il}*Addu* 5) ^{amel}*na-ya-li i-na* ^{al}*A-ri* 6) *ù bît-šu eqil*^{M}*-šu* 7) *ša* ^{I}*Ig-mar-*^{il}*Addu i-na* $^{al}{}_2$*Iṣṣur-be-li*

---

[1] For a special investigation of the term in Ugarit, with references to the earlier literature, cf. *M. Heltzer*, Penalties for Non-Performance of Obligations (the term *nayyālu* in Ugarit), VDI, 1971, No. 2, pp. 78–84 (Russian with English Summary); cf. also *J. N. Postgate*, Land Tenure in the Middle Assyrian Period; A reconstruction, BSOAS, 34, 1971, pp. 496–520, esp. pp. 508–12. Only three texts (KAU 160, 162, KAV 212) are known in which the term *nayyālu* appears. Although *J. N. Postgate* interprets this term as "a man with no living father and no male heirs," it is clear from the content of the texts that the *nayyālu* in Middle Assyria was, similar to the *nayyālu* found in the Ugaritic texts, a man deprived of his landholdings.

8) *ù i-din-šu a-na* ^{I}*Nu-ri-ya-na* 9) *ù bît-šu eqil*^{M}*-šu* 10) *ša* ^{I}*Bin-Bu-uk-ru-na* 11) *i-na* ^{al}*Ma-ra-pa* 12) *iš-ši-šu šarru ù id-din-šu* 13) *a-na* ^{I}*Nu-ri-ya-na a-na mârē*^{M}*-šu* 14) *a-na da-ri du-ri* 15) *ú-ra-am še-ra-am ma-am-ma-an* 16) *la i-le-qi iš-tu qâti*^{M} 17) *Nu-ri-ya-na (ù) iš-tu qâti*^{M} *[mârē*^{M}*]-šu*

"1) From the present day: 2) *Niqmaddu*, son of *Ammistamru*, 3) withdrew[2] the house, the fields, 4) (and) all that (as) *Igmaraddu* 5) the *nayyālu* in (the village) *Ari*, 6) and the house and field 7) of *Igmaraddu* in (the village) *Iṣṣur-be-li*. 8) And he gave it to *Nuriyanu*. 9) And the house (and) field 10) of ^{I}*Bin-Bukruna* 11) in (the village) *Marapa* 12) the king withdrew and gave it 13) to *Nuriyanu* and his sons 14) forever. 15) In the future nobody 16) (shall) take (away) from the hand 17) (of) *Nuriyanu* (and) from the hands of his [sons]."

At least one of the persons from whom the land was confiscated was a *nayyālu*. The profession of the persons who were deprived of land is not mentioned, but we know what villages their possessions were located in. We can thus assume that they could have been members of the rural community. It must be noted that *Nuriyanu* was a member of the royal family—the king's brother.[3]

2. PRU, III, 15.89.

The tablet begins with the standard formula and relates that king *Niqmaddu* (II), son of *Ammistamru:* 4) *it-ta-ši bît-šu eqil-šu* 5) *gab-ba mi-im-mi-šu* 6) *ša* ^{I}*Ili-ša-li-ma aḫi* ^{I}*Da-li-li* 7) ^{amel}*na-ya-li u id-din-šu* 8) *a-na* ^{f}*A-ḫa-ti-milku* 9) *mârat* ^{I}*Dalili* 10) *ú-ra-am še-ra-am* 11) *ḫa-aš-ḫa-at* ^{I}*A-ḫa-tum-milku* 12) *ù a-na* ^{I}*Nu-ri-iš-ti* 13) *ta-na-din-šu ḫa-aš-ḫa-at-ma* 14) *ù a-na mârē*^{M} ^{I}*Ya-ri-milku* 15) *ta-na-din-šu a-na sa-ak-nim bi-it-ša* 16) *ta-na-din-šu ú-ra-am še-ra-am* 17) *ma-am-ma-an la i-le-qi* 18) *iš-tu qâti*^{ti} ^{f}*A-ḫa-ti-milku* 19) *a-na da-ri du-ri* 20) *ù ú-nu-uš-ša bîti* 21) *up-pa-lu.*

"4) withdrew the house (and) field 5) together with all (property) 6) of *Ilišalima*, the brother of *Dalilu*, 7) the *nayyālu*, and gave it to the (woman) *Aḫatmilku*, 9) daughter of *Dalilu*. 10) (If) in the future 11) *Aḫatmilku* shall desire, 12) so she gives it to 13) *Nurištu*, and if she desires, 14) so she gives it 15) to the sons of 16) *Yarimilku* (and if she desires) she gives it to the *sākinu* of 17) her household. In future 18) nobody shall take (away) from the hands of *Aḫatmilku* 19) forever. 20) And the *unuššu*-service of her household 21) they have to perform."

This text relates that *Ilišalimu* was the *nayyālu*. It seems that his brother *Dalilu* was no longer living. The land was not taken away from

---

[2] For the term cf. above, pp. 50–51.

[3] Cf. *M. Heltzer*, Some Questions of the Agrarian Relations in Ugarit, VDI, 1960, No. 2, p. 89 (Russian).

the family since the king handed it over to the niece of *Ilišalimu*, the daughter of his brother. She had the land in her possession, but could not freely dispose of it. There were only three persons to whom she could hand over the land: a certain *Nurištu;* the sons of *Yarimilku;* or the *sākinu (skn)* of her household (majordomo). The mention of a majordomo indicates that the household under consideration was a large and wealthy one. It is possible that *Nurištu* and *Yarimilku* also had a close relationship to the same family. It is very important to note that the *unuššu*-corvée or service of the house had to be performed. This indicates that the land was not royal property, bound with some service, but that the lands had their obligations inside of the community.[4]

3. PRU, III, 16.174.

According to this text the same king, *Niqmaddu* II, withdrew the fields of 5) . . . *ITa-ki-ya-na mâr Ka-ma-li-ba-di* 6) *amelna-ya-li* 7) *ù id-din-šu* 8) *a-na ITup-pí-ya-na amelšatammi* 9) *išten en-šu ITup-pí-ya-nu* 10) *i-na 1 me-at 35 kaspi* 11) *il-te-qi-šu* 12) *i-na šimti qamirti: ṣu-um-mu-da* 13) *ù ša-na-am it-ta-ši-šu* 14) *šarru ù id-din-šu* 15) *a-na ITup-pí-ya-na* 16) *ú-ra-am še-ra-am* 17) *ma-am-ma-[a]n ú-ul i-laq-qi-šu* 18) *iš-t[u qâti ITup-pí-ya-na]* (the rest is broken).

"5) *Takiyanu*, son of *Kamalibadu*, 6) a *nayyālu*, 7) and gave it 8) to *Tuppiyanu*, the *šatammu*.[5] 9) First: *Tuppiyanu* 10) bought it 11) for 135 (sheqels) of silver 12) for the full price (it is granted). 13) And then the king 14) withdrew it and gave it 15) to *Tuppiyanu*. 16) In future 17) nobody shall not take it 18) fro[m the hands of *Tuppiyanu*] . . ."

The *šatammu*-official did not receive the land from the king as a gift for his service. Rather, he purchased it "for the full price." Thus, we see that the land confiscated from the *nayyālu* was not royal land but private property inside a certain unnamed village.

4. PRU, III, 16.262.

This text relates that King *Niqmaddu* II "withdrew the house, the fields, and all that he had from *Yašlimanu*, son of *Baalaṣi* 7) *amelna-ya-li* 8) *ù it-ta-din-šu* 9) *a-na IA-da-nu-um-mi* 10) *ù IA-da-nu-um-mu* 11) *pi-il-ka₄ ša bîti ú-bal* (Lines 12–15 contain the prohibition to deprive him and his children of the land).

---

4 On the *sākinu* of the household, cf. Ch. III, p. 50, note No. 8. On *unuššu* (Ug. *unṯ*), cf. with Akk. *ilku/pilku* from Ugarit; *M. Liverani*, Storia, pp. 140, 148–98; *M. Dietrich, O. Loretz*, Die soziale Struktur von Alalaḫ und Ugarit, I, Die Berufsbezeichnungen mit der hurritischen Endung *-ḫuli*, WO, III, 1966, No. 3, pp. 194–97.

5 On the functions and social position of the royal functionary *šatammu* in Ugarit, cf. *M. Heltzer*, Povinnostnoye Zemlevladeniye, pp. 191–92, esp. note No. 70; *Rainey*, Social Structure, pp. 34–35.

"7) the *nayyālu* 8) and gave it 9) to *Adanummu.* 10) And *Adanummu* 11) has to perform the *pilku*-service of his house(hold)."

Adanummu received the lands and immovables confiscated from *Yašlimanu,* the *nayyālu.* But *Adanummu* had to perform the service of the house(hold). The difference between this text and PRU, III, 15.89 (cf. above) lies only in the designation of the service as pilku, whereas in PRU, III, 15.89 we have the term *unuššu.* But the fact that the service had to be performed for the household shows, that the *nayyālu,* as well as the recipient, were villagers, members of the rural community.[6]

5. PRU, III, 15.168.

This text relates that king *Ammistamru* II 4) *it-ta-ši bîta ša* [I]*Qa-tu-na* 5) [ame]l*na-ya-li ša i-na* al*Rêši* 6) *ù it-ta-di-in-šu* 7) *a-na* f*Qi-ri-bi-li* 8) *ù i-na-an-na* f*Qi-ri-bi-lu* 9) *ti-ir-ta-ṣi-ip* 10) *bîta an-na[-a]* (Lines 11–17, standard formula of ownership; 18–21, the seal of the king and name of the scribe).

"4) withdrew the house of *Qatuna* 5) the *nayyālu* in (the village) *Rêšu* 6) and gave it 7) to (the woman) *Qiribilu.* 8) And therefore *Qiribilu* shall 9) rebuild 10) this house . . ."[7]

It is very interesting that the *nayyālu* who was a villager from *Rêšu* could neither perform his obligations nor keep his house in order. The woman *Qiribilu* was obligated to rebuild the house. No mention of special obligations appears in the text, but it seem that Qiribilu had the economic means to rebuild the house and to perform her obligations in the community.

6. PRU, III, 15.141.

This tablet declares that *Ammistamru* II withdrew the fields of *Kurbanu* "5) son of *Niltanu,* the *nayyālu,* 6) which lay among the fields of (the village) *Ṣau* 7) together with its *dimtu* (buildings), 8) with its olive trees, 9) with its vineyards, 10) with all that he has." (The text goes on to describe additional land confiscations (lines 11–12), but the end of the tablet is broken.) It is clear from this text that a villager was deprived of his land.

7. U, V, 9 (RS. 17.61).

This tablet differs to a great extent from the texts given above and it aids in obtaining important additional data about the *nayyālu*—former members of the village-community in the kingdom of Ugarit.

[6] Texts about withdrawal of lands from *nayyālu,* but it is unclear whether these are villagers or royal servicemen. Cf. also PRU, III, 15.145, 15.122; and the fragmentary text, PRU, III, 16.86 . . . 7' *[]qa-ni*amel*na-ya-li i-na* al*Bîri.*

[7] Cf. PRU, VI, 28 (RS. 17.39), where, in the badly damaged part of the text, 4) *[. . .]š[a] i-na* al*Rêši* 5) *[i]a-na(?)* amel*na-ya-lu,* appears.

1) *iš-tu ûmi*^{mi} *an-ni-im* 2) *a-na pa-ni* ^{amel}*šîbûte*^{te} 3) ^{I}*I-ri-bi-ilu* ^{amel}*sākin (MAŠKIM)* ^{al}*Riq-di* 4) *it-ta-ši bîta eqla*^{M} *gáb-bá mi-i[m-m]i-ši-na* 5) *ša mârat Ya-ak-ni ù ša mâra[t X]-ab-i* 6) ^{amel}*na-ya-lu-ti* 7) *ù it-ta-din-š[u] a-n[a]* ^{I}*Abdi-*^{il}*Yaraḫ mâr Ku-um-*^{d}*U* 8) *i-na 3 me-at kas[pi]* 9) *eqlu*^{M} *ṣamid* 10) *ur-ra še-ra-am* 11) *ma-an-nu-um-ma* 12) *ú-ul i-leq[-qi-š]u* 13) *iš-tu qâti* ^{I}*Abdi-*^{il}*Yaraḫ* 14) *ù qâti mârē*^{M}*-šu* 15) *šîbu* ^{I}*Tup-pi-ya-nu mâr Ar-sú-wa-na* 16) *šîbu* ^{I}*I-mi-da-nu mâr Ku-za-na* 17) *šîbu* ^{I}*Abdu mâr Abdi-*^{il}*Rašap* 18) *šîbu* ^{I}*Ili-*^{il}*Rašap mâr Tu-ba-na* 19) *šîbu* ^{I}*Abdi-*^{il}*Rašap mâr Tub-bi-te-na* 20) *šîbu* ^{I}*Abdi-a-šar-ti mâr Ya-an-ḫa-am-mi* 21) ^{aban}*kunuk* ^{I}*I-ri-bi-ili* 22) ^{I}*Ilu-milku* ^{amel}*ṭupšarru*

"1) From the present day, 2) before witnesses, 3) *Iribilu*, the *sakinu* of (the village) *Riqdu*, 4) withdrew the house (and) the fields (and) what they (women) possess, 5) of the daughter of *Yaknu* and the daught[er of *x]abi*, 6) the *nayyālu* (women) 7) and he gave i[t t]o *Abdiyaraḫ*, son of *Kum-U*[8] 8) for 300 (sheqels) of sil[ver]. 9) The fields are bound. 10) In the future 11) nobody 12) shall ta[ke] them away 13) from the hands of *Abdiyaraḫ* 14) and from his sons. 15) Witness: *Tuppiyanu*, son of *Arsuwanu*. 16) Witness: *Imidanu*, son of *Kuzanu*. 17) Witness: *Abdu*, son of *Abdirašap*. 18) Witness: *Ilirašap*, son of *Tubanu*. 19) Witness: *Abdirašap*, son of *Tubbitenu*. 20) Witness: *Abdiašarti*, son of *Yanḫammu*. 21) Seal of *Iribilu*. 22) *Ilumilku*, the scribe."[9]

Contrary to the text composed in the name of the king, this text is written in the presence of witnesses and in the name of *Iribilu*, the *sākinu* of the village *Riqdi*,[10] who was the representative of the royal administration. The land was taken away from two women. Perhaps they were widows and had no manpower in their households for performing the regular obligations connected with their lands. (Cf. note No. 1, p. 52.) It is clear that the representative of the local royal authorities had the right to deprive the *nayyālu* of their lands. The new landowner, *Abdiyaraḫ*, had to pay 300 sheqels of silver and, as in former cases, the recipient paid the full price of the land. Finally, this text shows clearly that the *nayyālu*

---

[8] Theophoric name, but it is unclear which deity appears under the ideogramm ^{d}*U*.

[9] Cf. also, the fragmentary part of PRU, VI, 55 (RS. 18.22), 5') *ù eqlātu*^{M} *ša* ^{f}*Ḫa-mé-en-na-ya-* 6') ^{amel}*na-ya-li sa i-na eqlāt*^{M} $^{il}{}_{2}$*Ištar*. ("5') and the field of (the woman) *Ḫamenaya*, 6') the *nayyālu*, which is among the fields of (the goddess) Istar.") Although this is not entirely clear, we see that among the *nayyālu* there appears again a woman.

[10] About the *sākinu* of a village, cf. *M. Heltzer*, Carskaya administraciya i dvorcovy personal v Ugarite, LAMMD, X, 1969, (Russian), p. 228; cf. below, p. 82.

in various villages were members of the rural community. The royal authorities, after confiscating the lands of the *nayyālu* in the villages, 1) delivered them, for a certain price, to people who had to take on themselves the obligations of the disowned member of the rural community, or b) handed the land over to royal servicemen as a holding for their service. But we must keep in mind that royal servicemen who did not perform their obligations could also become *nayyālu*. The texts dealing with royal servicemen *nayyālu* are not given here.

It is obvious that land confiscation from the *nayyālu* who were members of the rural community was one of the sources of enriching the crown and the treasury. The only way for a *nayyālu* to survive, once deprived of land, was to enter into royal service and to become a "royal dependent" *(bnš mlk)*.

The Enslavement of Rural Debtors by Foreign Tamkars

Sometimes, as we have seen above, the villagers lost their land for non-performance of their obligations. But this was not the only means of dealing with debtors. We have the following declaration of the Hittite king Hattusilis III, concerning the activities of the city of Ura in Asia Minor in Ugarit. (PRU, IV, 17.130.)

25) *ù šum-ma kaspu*^{M} *ša mârē*^{M} ^{al}*U-ra* 26) *it-ti mârē* ^{al}*Ú-ga-ri-it* 27) *ù a-na šu-lu-mi-šu la-a i-le-u* 28) *ù šár* ^{mat}*Ú-ga-ri-it amêlu*^{lim} *ša-a-šu* 29) *qa-du aššati-šu qa-du mârē*^{M}*-šu* 30) *i-na qâti*^{ti} *mârē* ^{al}*U-ra* 31) *amêl*^{M} *tamkāri i-na-an-di-in-šu-nu-ti.*

"25) And if silver of the sons of Ura 26) is with the sons of Ugarit, 27) and they are not able to repay it, 28) so the king of Ugarit these people 29) together with his wife, together with his sons, 30) into the hands of 31) the merchant shall deliver."

It is clear from this text that, at least in some cases, the foreign *tamkars* had the right to enslave the "sons of Ugarit," i.e. people of various villages of this country. It is noteworthy that the foreigners had no right to acquire the lands of these people, which remained in the hands of the king of Ugarit.[11]

---

[11] *Liverani*, Storia, pp. 80–86; *M. Heltzer*, Slaves, Slave-owning, and the Role of Slavery in Ugarit, VDI, 1968, No. 3, 12.91 (Russian with English summary); *M. Heltzer*, The *tamkar* and his role in Western Asia in the XIV–XIII centuries, B.C., VDI, 1964, No. 2, pp. 7–8 (Russian); *R. Yaron*, Foreign Merchants in Ugarit, ILR, IV, 1969, pp. 71–74.

We know also, that "the sons of Ugarit were delivered to other countries for their silver,"[12] and can assume that these rural citizens were debtors unable to repay their debts.

Defection of the Peasants of Ugarit

It is natural that developments such as those described above created tendencies to leave home and seek refuge in neighbouring countries or kingdoms, as well as in other places of the same country. The tendency to defection at this time were brilliantly clarified in a recent study by M. Liverani.[13] The main bulk of M. Liverani's study is devoted to clarifying the social character of the *ḫapiru (SA.GAZ)* people and investigating the tendency toward nomadisation. Our data from Ugarit, and especially from PRU, VI, shed light on this tendency inside Ugarit. There are even instances where the documents available deal with concrete situations and individuals.

Text PRU, IV, 17.238[14] deals with the "sons of Ugarit" (line 4), among other social categories of the people of Ugarit. The text relates that: "sons of Ugarit, (who) are delivered for their silver (debts) to another country, and from (the land) of Ugarit they are fleeing . . . and entering the (territory of the) *ḫapiru* . . ." Such defection could occur for political reasons, or, as we have seen above, for material reasons. We possess a certain number of texts in which the guarantors of certain persons are instructed to pay large sums to the king in case the persons who received the guaranty flees to another country.[15] We know from the same texts, that some of the refugees were seized and returned to their country of origin.

Even more interesting is the second part of the text, which confirms that sometimes citizens of Ugarit—people of the villages of Ugarit—were delivered to their creditors from abroad as slaves.[16] It may be that such people were the *nayyālu*, people who did not, or could not perform all their obligations.[17]

---

[12] Cf. PRU, IV, 17.238, the text translation, cf. Ch. I pp. 4–5.

[13] *Liverani*, Il fuoroscitismo in Siria nella tardo eta del Bronzo, RSI, LXXVII, 1965, No. 2, pp. 315–36.

[14] Chapter I, pp. 4–5.

[15] Cf. PRU, III, 15.81, p. 37; 16.287, p. 37; PRU, IV, 17.315, p. 111; 17.341, p. 161; 18.04, p. 241; 17.369A, p. 51; PRU, VI, 68 (RS. 17.84), p. 63; 69 (RS. 17.329), p. 64.

[16] Cf. PRU, IV, 17.130; cf. above, p. 57.

[17] *Heltzer*, Penalties; cf. also, part 1 of this chapter.

Let us consider the more detailed texts from PRU, VI which deal with particular cases. (The defection of representatives of the upper classes for political reasons are not under consideration here.)

A small tablet, PRU, VI, 76 (RS. 17.361), relates: 1) *ṭup-pu an-nu-ú ša amêlē*^{M} 2) *mu-un-na⟨-ab⟩-ṭu-ti.*[18] "1) This tablet (concerns) the persons, 2) who are defectors." The scribe evidently did not intend to give a list of the defectors since the tablet has no room for one. In contrast, PRU, VI, 77 (RS. 19.32) contains a letter concerning refugees, sent by one royal official to another.

1) ^{I}*Ša-m[a]-nu ša ta-ba-'a*	"1) *Sam[a]nu* whom you search for
2) $^{[a]l}$*Ma-ag-da-la*	2) (is in the) village *Magdala,*
3) ^{I}*Su-a-nu-a-nu ù [*^{I}*Ḫ]e-bat-*^{il}*Šapaš*	3) *Suanuanu* and *[Ḫ]ebatšapaš,*
4) *ša i[q]a-bu*[19] ^{al}*Ap-su-na il-ka la-lak*[20]	4) who are said (to be in the) village *Apsuna* (and) did not perform their corvée.[21]
5) ^{I}*Aš-ta-bi-šarru* ^{al}*Ḫar-ga-na-a ú-šab*	5) *Aštabišarru* is in the village *Ḫarganu.*
6) ^{I}*Ibri*^{ri}*-za-zu* ^{al}*Bi-ta-ḫu-li ú-šab*	6) *Ibrizazu* is[22] in the village *Bitaḫuli.*
7) ^{I}*Na-zi-ya-a-nu* ^{al}*Ša-am-ra-a KIMIN*	7) *Naziyanu* (the same) in the village *Šamra*
8) *napḫar 6 ṣâbū*^{M}	8) Together 6 warriors (soldiers)[23]
9) *la-li-ku ša il-ki*	9) who went not to their (conscription) duty,
10) ^{al}*Ap-su-ni-ya-ma*	10) Apsunites."

This text lists six villagers of *Apsuna*, a well-known Ugaritic village, who did not perform their conscription duty.[24] The author of the text

[18] The scribal omission is reconstructed by *J. Nougayrol.*

[19] *iqabū*—plural.

[20] *la-lak* from *lā il-lak,* cf. U,V, 96 (RS. 20.12) *lā ša-li-ma* ("did not pay," "did not perform (the duty)").

[21] Or "duty."

[22] The verb *wašābu* can be interpreted as being in a certain place at the moment, also a permanent dwelling.

[23] *J. Nougayrol*, PRU, VI, p. 75, translates, "travailleurs (ou: soldats)" but by comparison with text PRU, VI, 95 (RS. 19.74), where the term *ṣâbū* appears fragmented, and which relates details about conscription-duty from the villages of Ugarit, we prefer "warriors," or "soldiers," cf. Ch. II, pp. 19–21; cf. *Rainey*, IOS, III, 1973, pp. 40–41, where the author gives a slightly different interpretation of the text, supposing that the six villagers tried to escape from their feudal services.

[24] About the conscription of villagers of Ugarit, cf. *M. Heltzer*, Soziale Aspekte des Heerwesens in Ugarit, BSSAV, Berlin, 1971, p. 130; cf. also, Ch. II, pp. 19–22.

instructs another official where to search for hiding men. *Magdala* (Ug. *Mgdly*),[25] *Bitaḫuli*,[26] *Šamra* (Ug. *Ṯmr(y)*),[27] are well known villages of the kingdom of Ugarit. We also know that *Magdala* and *Bitaḫuli* were border-villages of the kingdom. *Ḫargana* occurs here for the first time in the published documents. Concerning two individuals (lines 3–4), we know only that they did not perform their duty; it was not known where they were hiding. We can assume from the text that the people, who wanted to escape conscription, successfully disappeared. The other persons mentioned in the text were located in villages of the kingdom of Ugarit, but these villages were near to the border of the kingdom and their intention may have been to defect abroad.

A text similar to that given above is PRU, VI, 78 (RS. 19.41). The last lines of this text (25–26) show that it is dealing with 25) *amêlu*^{M} ^{al}*Qa-ra-ti-ya-ma i[-na gá]b-bu* 26) *âlāni*$^{D.D.M.}$ ^{mat}*Si-e-a-ni*. "25) People of the village *Qaratu* (who are) in 26) the villages of the land of *Siannu*."[27a] Siannu was a country bordering on Ugarit, and subservient to it until the time of the Hittite king, Mursili II. Mursili II freed Siannu from subservience to Ugarit. Thereafter, Siannu paid annual tribute to the king of Karkhemiš, where princes of the Hittite royal dynasty ruled.[28] The text mentions by name twenty-three persons from the well-known Ugaritic village *Qaratu*. They dwelled (u-šab) in the villages of: 1) ^{al}*Gi-ma-ni*, 2) ^{al}*La-š[a]-be*, 3) ^{al}*Si-il-la-[x]*, 4) ^{al}*Du-ma-te-qi*, *(Du-ma-te*^{KI}*)* 5) ^{al}*Mu-ur-ša-a*, 6) ^{al}*Ga-li-li-tu-ki-ya*, 7) ^{al}*Šam-ra-a*,[29] 8) ^{al}*Qi-mi-ṣu*, 9) ^{al}*Šá-ba-a-ili*, 10) ^{al}*Ṣa-'u*, 11) ^{al}*Mar-du-še*, 12) ^{al}*Am-me-šá-be*, 13) ^{al}*Ar-me-lu* (seven persons), 14) ^{al}*Ma-ra-ilu*.

Listed here are fourteen villages to which men of *Qaratu* defected. But the text raises a problem. Six villages, ^{al}*Du-ma-te-qi*,[30] ^{al}*Ga-li-la-tu-ki-ya*

---

[25] Cf. PRU, II, 81 (UT. 1081), 10; PRU, IV, 17.62, 6; 17.366, 16; PRU, V, 44 (UT, 2044), 11; 145 (UT, 2145); U,V, 102 (RS. 20.207 A), 10.

[26] Var. *Bi-ta-ḫu-li-wi*, PRU, IV, 17.62, 1; 17.366, 12.

[27] CTC, 69, 4 (UT. 111); 71, 20 (UT, 113); PRU, II, 81 (UT, 1081), 4; 181 (UT, 1971), 13; PRU, V, 44 (UT, 2044), 8; 58, II (UT, 2058), 37; PRU, VI, 105 (RS. 19. 117), 8; 111 (RS. 19.129), 6.

[27a] *Rainey*, IOS, III, 1973, pp. 41–42 gives a similar explanation of these lines without entering into the meaning of the text in general.

[28] *Liverani*, Storia, pp. 72–73, with references to the sources.

[29] *Nougayrol*, PRU, VI, p. 75, gives the reading *Ú-ra-a*, but the town *Ura* was, as we know, located in Asia Minor and not in the vicinity of Ugarit. Inside the kingdom of Ugarit we know of ^{al}*Šamra (Ṯmry)*. The *ú* sign also has the reading *šam*. So *Šamra* is preferable.

[30] PRU, VI, 138 (RS. 19.46), 16; cf. also, table No. 1.

(Ug. *Glltky*),[31] ^{al}*Šam-ra-a* (Ug. *T̲mry*),[32] ^{al}*Qi-mi-ṣu* (Ug. *Qmṣ*),[33] ^{al}*Ṣa-'u* (Ug. *Ṣ*^{c}),[34] and ^{al}*Ma-ra-ilu* (Ug. *Mril*),[35] are well-known as villages of the kingdom of Ugarit. (The other place-names could really be villages of the kingdom of Siannu.) At the same time, we have no reason to doubt that if the document designates these *âlu* as villages of the kingdom of Siannu, it is not really so. In connection with this problem arises another problem, that of the datation of the text PRU, VI, 78. Knowing that Siannu was freed from the sovereignity of Ugarit in the last years of Mursili II, the first years of *Niqmepa*, King of Ugarit, we can assume that this tablet dates from no later than 1315 B.C.E.[36]

On the other hand, the texts PRU, V, 74, 77, and 90, which mention *Qmṣ*, *Ṣ*^{c} and *Mril*, came from the tablet-baking furnace and therefore belong to the very last years of the existence of Ugarit. During this period these *âlu/qrit* belonged to the kingdom of Ugarit. The text PRU, III, 15.155, concerning *Ṣa-'u* is dated by the reign of *Ammistamru* II, as are PRU, III, 15.140, 15.141, and 16.131. We see that *Ṣa'u*, at least, was within the confines of the kingdom of Ugarit during the reign of *Ammistamru* II. We must therefore assume that the six *âlu* mentioned in the text as belonging to Siannu were subdued by Ugarit only during the period following the reign of Mursili II (died ca. 1315 b.c.), during the reign of Niqmeqa of Ugarit (reigned until ca. 1265 b.c.), and until the beginning of the reign of *Ammistamru* II (reigned until ca. 1230 b.c.), son of Niqmepa. At least at the time of *Ammistamru* II, the kingdom of Siannu did not cease to exist. But Ugarit probably enlarged its own domains at the expense of Siannu. Thus, the text concerning refugees from Ugarit gives us very important chronological evidence.[37]

The principal difference between the texts PRU, VI, 77 and 78 lies in the fact that PRU, VI, 77 concerns people who defected from their own village to other villages in the same country, while PRU, VI, 78 deals

---

[31] PRU, V, 42. Tr. 2 (UT, 2041); 118, 8–9 (UT, 2118).

[32] Cf. Note No. 29.

[33] PRU, V, 74, 14 (UT, 2074).

[34] CTC, 67, 5 (UT, 116); 71, 4 (UT, 113); PRU, III, 15.141, 12; 15.182, 5; 16.150, 11; 16.277, 6; 15.155, 5; 15.140, 5; 15.142, 6; 16.131, 6; PRU, V, 40, 14 (UT, 2040); 77, 4 (UT, 2077); 146, 2 (UT, 2146); U,V, 6 (RS. 17.149); 159 (RS. 17.86).

[35] CTC, 71, 51 (UT, 113); PRU, III, 11.830, 10; PRU, IV, 17.62, 25; 17.340, v, 7; PRU, V, 48, 22 (UT, 2048); 90, 9 (UT, 2090); 144, 1 (UT, 2144).

[36] Cf. *Liverani*, Storia, Tavola I; *Klengel*, Geschichte Syriens, 2, Berlin, 1969, p. 455.

[37] Cf. PRU, VI, for full evidence including all available data; cf. U, V, about the reign of Niqmepa and Ammistamru II, also *Klengel*, Geschichte Syriens, II, Berlin, 1969, pp. 361–388.

with persons who defected to the neighbouring kingdom. Taking into account the evidence given at the beginning of this paper about refugees who defected to the territories under the direct rule of the Hittite king, we have to conclude that the heavy burden of taxes, duties, conscriptions and debt caused the defection of villagers from the kingdom of Ugarit to other places in the same country, to neighbouring countries, or to territories under direct control of the Hittite king.[38] This is aside from defections caused by political struggles and attempts to seek asylum.

The texts referred to above illustrate cases in which villagers became *nayyālu*, were enslaved to foreign creditors for their debts, or defected. Defections may have been prompted by fear of enslavement, or fear of conscription. Defection may also have been an alternative to the burden of taxes, corvée-service, and other obligations. These texts seem to indicate that every villager was known to the authorities as a member of a particular village-community.

[38] PRU, VI, 80 (RS. 19.111), containing a list of various persons, dwelling in various *âlu*, but does not make clear whether they were refugees or not.

CHAPTER V

OTHER ASPECTS OF COMMUNITY LIFE IN UGARIT

The royal authorities in Ugarit had both the power and the skill to impose their demands on the rural communities. However, there were customs and traditions which protected the village-community from ruination. Using all the available material, we will try to elucidate the manifold life of this social body—the rural community.

Collective Responsibility in Legal Actions

The rural communities were collectively responsible for corvée, conscription, taxes, etc. They were also collectively responsible in various legal actions.

Text PRU, IV, 17.229 relates that, "in the village of *Apsuna* was killed"[1] a royal *tamkar* of *Talimmu*, king of a small state not far from Ugarit. The murder took place because *Talimmu* "raised a legal case with the sons of *Apsuna*."[2] The outcome was that the "sons of *Apsuna*" had to pay "1 talent of silver"[3] to *Talimmu*.

In PRU, IV, 17.288 the king of the neighbouring kingdom, *Ušnatu*, demanded from the *sākinu* of Ugarit[4] an investigation of "the sons of *Araniya* . . . for the slaves filled the hands of the sons of *Araniya* with stolen (property)."[5]

The state of preservation of PRU, IV, 17.299 is very poor, but we can discern that a certain "*Qadidu* brought a legal case againtst the sons of *Ḫalbi rapši*,"[6] because his brother was killed in that village.[7]

U, V, 52 (RS. 20.239) is a most outstanding text, which is in a good state of preservation.

[1] *i-na* ^{al}*Ap-su-na-a di-ku*$_{8}$*-u-mi.*

[2] *it-ti mârē*^{M} ^{al}*Ap-su-na a-na di-ni iq-ri-bu.*

[3] *1 bilat kaspu[ ].* 1 talent in Ugarit equalled about 28 kilograms', *N. F. Parise*, Per uno studio del sistema . . ., pp. 21–23; cf. also PRU, IV, 17.369B, where the people of *Apsuna* are shown also to bear collective responsibility for a murder, but the text is severely damaged and the details of the document are illegible.

[4] *Heltzer*, Carskaya administraciya (Royal Administration), pp. 224–27.

[5] 8) *dînūti*^{M}*-ti š[a] mârē*^{M} ^{al}*A-ra-ni-ya* 9) *ip-ru-sum-mu* . . . 21) *ki-i-me-e ardu*^{M} *ša-ra-qa i-na qa-ti mârē*^{M} ^{al}*A-ra-ni-ya* 22) *u-ma-la-u.*

[6] 2) ^{I}*Qa-di-du it-ti mârē*^{M} ^{al}*Ḫal-bi rapši* 3) *[a]-na di-ni iš-ni-qu.*

[7] 5) . . . *aḫu-ya* ("my brother") *[i-na* ^{al}*Ḫal-bi rapsi (?)] di-ku-ni[ ].* It seems that an answer of the people of *Ḫalbi rapši* followed.

1) *um-ma* ^{I}*Ma-da-'-e*	"1) So *Mada'e*
2) *a-na* ^{amel}*sà-ki-ni*	2) to the *sākinu*[8]
3) *qi-bi-ma*	3) says
4) *lu-ú šul-mu a-na muḫ-ḫi-ka*	4) Peace to You!
5) *ilânu*^{M} *a-na šul-ma-ni*	5) The gods for health
6) *liṣṣuru*^{ru}*-ka*	6) May guard You!
7) *aššum alpu*^{M}*-ya ša il-tar-qu*	7) Concerning my oxen, which the men of
8) *amêlu*^{M} *âl Ra-ak-b[a-y]a*	8) *Rakba* had stolen:
9) *kí-i táq-ta-b[i*	9) According to what You sai[d
10) *ma-a ki-i-me-e [šarru(?)]*	10) "That alike [the king(?)] . . .
11) *iš-tu* ^{m}*[*^{at}*Ugarit?]*	11) from th[e land of Ugarit?]
12) *il-la-[ak]*	12) he go[es?] (he would go?)[9]
13) *šu-up-ra-a[m-mi(?)]*	13) Ask m[e (personally) (or "demand")
14) *di-na ša alpi*^{M}*[-ka(?)]*	14) (on) the legal case concerning [Your?] oxen[9a]
15) *lu ga-mi-ir-[mi]*	15) So we will finish it.
16) *i-na-an-na di-na ša-a[-š(?)]i*	16) Further: Th[is] legal case:
17) *gu*$_5$*-mi-ir alpē*^{M}*-ya*	17) All my oxen
18) *li-te-ru-ni-in-ni*	18) — (who) has to return them me?
19) *ù šum-ma alpē*^{M}*-ya*	19) And if my oxen
20) *la-a i-na-di-nu-ni*	20) shall not be returned
21) $^{\text{amelM}}{}_2$*šîbūtu*^{M} *ša* ^{al}*Ra-ak-ba*	21) (So) the elders of *Rakba:*
22) ^{I}*Ba-bi-ya-nu*	22) *Babiyanu,*
23) *mâr* ^{I}*Ya-du-da-na*	23) son of *Yadudana,*
24) ^{I}*Ab-du qa-du* ^{I}*mâri-šu*	24) *Abdu* together with his son,
25) *ù* ^{I}*Ad-du-nu*	25) and *Addunu,*
26) ^{amel}*ḫa-at-ni-šu*	26) his son-in-law
27) *ù* ^{amel}*akil li-im*	27) and the head of the thousand[10]
28) *amêlu*^{M} *an-nu-tu*$_4$ *lil-l[i]ku-ni*	28) — these people sha[ll] go
29) *[a]-(?)-na bît ilim*^{lim} *li-ru-bu*	29) (and) enter the sanctuary,[11]
30) *u lu-ú za-ku-ú*	30) and they are free (from obligations)"

[8] The *sākinu*, vizier, of the kingdom of Ugarit.

[9] All reconstructions of the texts are made by the editor, *J. Nougayrol.*

[9a] *Berger*, UF, II, 1970, p. 290 *alpi*^{ME}*[*^{Š}*-ia].*

[10] A military rank in Ugarit; cf. also PRU, VI, 52 (RS. 19,78), 4.

[11] In order to give the oath; *Berger*, UF, II, p. 290 reads the beginning of the line *di-na-an e[. . .*

The above text shows that people of *Rakba* were collectively responsible for the stolen oxen and that the only way to prove they were not guilty was to give an oath in the sanctuary. The oath had to be given by the elders of the *âlu*, in the name of the whole population of this village.

The data available from the various texts shows us that every theft, murder, or other crime committed by people of a certain village, or inside the territory of a village, was the collective responsibility of the citizens of that village. Perhaps this occurred only in cases where no criminal was named or apprehended by the authorities. The village had to free herself from responsibility through oathgiving, or some other act, performed by its representatives, the elders of the village. The data thus shows, once more, the communal organization of the *âlu/qrt* in Ugarit.

Communal Landowning and Landholding by the Rural Community[12]

It would be difficult to assume that the rural community in Ugarit was so primitive that it possessed land which was collectively worked by its people. But it seems very likely that the community had certain rights and jurisdiction over the lands of its members. At the same time, the king had certain rights over the community. But the mere fact that the king addresses the village *(âlu)* as a single body, brings the whole issue into the confines of communal organization.

This is treated in text PRU, III, 16.170. Only the reverse of the tablet is partly preserved. Lines 1'–3' of the text deal with *Abdianati*, king of the neighbouring Siyannu. This is followed by:

4') *[ù eqlāt]*^{M} ^{al}*Ḫa-ar-ma-na* 5') *[ša u]l-tu da-ri-ti* 6') *[ša i-]na qâti amêlē*^{M} ^{al}*Mu-lu-uk-ki* 7') *[i-n]a qâti*^{M}*-ma amêlē*^{M} ^{al}*Mu-lu-uk-[ki]* 8') *ù eqlāt*^{M} ^{al}*Ḫa-ar-ma-na* 9') *ša ul-tu da-ri-ti* 10') *ša i-na qâti amêlē*^{M} ^{al}*Gal-ba* 11') *i-na qâti*^{ti}*-ma amêlē*^{M} ^{al}*Gal-ba* 12') ^{aban}*kunuk* ^{I}*Niq-me-pa mâr Niq-ma-*^{il}*Addu* 13') *[šàr]* ^{al}*Ú-ga-ri-it*.

"4') [and the field]s (lands) of (the village) *Ḫarmanu* 5') [which fr]om ever 6') [were i]n the hands of the people of (the village) *Mulukku* 7') (shall be) [i]n the hands of the people of (the village) *Muluk[ku]*. 8') And the fields of (the village) *Ḫarmanu* 9') which from ever 10') were in the hands of the people of (the village) *Galba* 11') (shall be) in the hands

---

[12] Cf. *I. M. Diakonoff*, Problems of Property. The Structure of Near Eastern Society to the Middle of the Second Millenium B.C. (Russian with English summary), VDI, 1967, No. 4, pp. 13–35; ibid., The Rural Community in the Ancient Near East, JESHO, XVIII, 1975, pp. 121–33.

of the people of (the village) *Galba*. 12') Seal of *Niqmepa*, son of *Niqmaddu*, 13') [king] of Ugarit."

The remnants of this text correspond to a great extent with PRU, IV, 17.123.

1) *iš-tu ûmi an-ni-im* 2) *di-nu-tu*$_4$ *eqlāt*^{M} ^{al}*Šu-uk-si* 3) *ù di-na-tu*$_4$ *eqlāt*^{M} ^{al}*Ḫa-ar-ma-na* 4) *i-da-i-nu a-na pa-ni* ^{il}*Šamši*^{ši} 5) *ù i-na-an-na iš-ku-nu* 6) *ki-it-ta i-na be-ri-šu-nu* 7) *ki-i-ma da-ri-i-ti* 8) *eqlāt*^{M} *šàr* ^{al}*Ú-ga-ri-it* 9) *ša i-na* 10) *ša ul-tu*$_4$ *da-ri-ti* 11) *a-na qâti*^{ti}*-ma šàr* ^{al}*Ú-ga-ri-it* 12) *ù eqlāt*^{M} *šàr* ^{al}*Ú-ga-ri-it* 13) *ša i-na eqlāt*^{M} ^{al}*Ḫa-ar-ma-na* 14) *ša ul-tu*$_4$ *da-ri-ti* 15) *a-na qâti*^{ti}*-ma šàr* ^{al}*Ú-ga-ri-it* 16) *ù eqlāt*^{M} ^{I}*Abdi-*^{il}*Ninurta* 17) *ša ul-tu*$_4$ *da-ri-ti* 18) *ša i-na* ^{al}*Šu-uk-si* 19) *a-na qâti*^{ti}*-ma* ^{I}*Abdi-*^{il}*Ninurta* 20) *ù eqlāt*^{M} ^{al}*Ḫa-ar-ma-na* 21) *ša ul-tu*$_4$ *da-ri-ti* 22) *ša a-na qâti*^{ti} ^{I}*Abdi-*^{il}*Ninurta* 23) *a-na qâti*^{ti}*-ma* ^{I}*Abdi-*^{il}*Ninurta* 24) ^{aban}*kunuk* ^{I}*Abdi-*^{il}*Ninurta* 25) *šàr* ^{al}*Si-ya-ni* 26) *ur*$_5$*-ra še-ra amêlum a-na amêlim* 27) *la i-ta-ur.*

"1) From the present day 2) the legal case (about) the fields of (the village) *Šuksi* 3) and the legal case (about) the fields of (the village) *Ḫarmanu* 4) was settled in the presence of the Sun (the great Hittite king). 5) And so he ruled: 6) Justice between them 7) as forever (let there be). 8) The fields of the king of Ugarit, 9) which are in *Šuksi*, 10) (and) which were fromever 11) in the hands of the king of Ugarit; 12) and the fields of the king of Ugarit, 13) which are among the fields of (the village) *Ḫarmanu*, 14) which were (his) fromever 15) shall remain in the hands of the king of Ugarit, 16) and the fields of *Abdininurta*, 17) which were fromever, 18) and are (located) in (the village) *Šuksi*, 19) in the hands of *Abdininurta*, 20) and the fields of (the village) *Ḫarmanu* 21) which were fromever 22) in the hands of *Abdininurta* 23) shall remain in the hands of *Abdininurta*. 24) Seal of *Abdininurta*, 25) king of Siyannu. 26) In future nobody shall 27) return (to this issue)."

We see from PRU, III, 16.170 that certain lands in the village *Ḫarmanu* were at the disposal of the people of two villages—*Mulukku* and *Galba*. This fact is significant because it means that a) people of a certain village could have lands in another village, b) these lands were under some kind of collective administration or management by the "people" *(mârē*^{M}*)* of the villages of *Mulukku* and *Galba*.

Text PRU, IV, 17.123 has more relation to political affairs. It deals with the arbitration of the Hittite king between the kings of Ugarit and Siyannu. We see that there were royal lands of both kings in the villages of *Šuksi* and *Ḫarmanu*. Both kings remained owners of these lands despite certain political changes in these villages. (It is not definitively clear whether these villages were under the sovereignty of Ugarit or Siyannu at that period.) It is important to note, that *Ḫarmanu*, mentioned in both texts, included royal lands, as well as communal lands of the villagers of *Mulukku* and *Galba*. The division between royal and communal lands is definitively clear in this text.

The analysis of PRU, III, 16.170 and IV, 17.123 helps us to understand a number of texts, written in alphabetic Ugaritic and dealing with land owned or held in one village by people of another village. Thus, PRU, V, 26 (UT, 2026) relates: 1) *šd. Snrym. dt. ᶜqb.* 2) *b. Ayly.* "1) The fields of the people (of the village) *Snr*, which are (located)[13] 2) in the village *Ayly*." This is followed by six lines (3–8) mentioning six fields, together with the names of their owners or holders, who are men of *Snr*. Line 9) *šd. bn. Ṯmr[n. M]idḫy* ("field of *bn Ṯmr[n]* man of (the village *[M]idḫ*") is of special interest. Perhaps he also had a field in *Ayly*. Thus, six fields of "men of *Snr*," and one field of a "man of *Midḫ*,"[14] were located in the village *Ayly*. This is strikingly similar to the data from PRU, III, 16.170.

The question now arises: how could people of one village have their lands in another village? It seems unlikely that they purchased the land, for they did not get their rights as "sons" *(mârē*ᴹ*)* of the second village. They remained "sons" of their original village. Perhaps they received certain holdings in villages where depopulation had taken place as a result of war, epidemic, or defection of the villagers (cf. above, Ch. IV).

PRU, V, 29 (UT, 2029) may shed light on this problem.

This text deals with landholdings *(ubdy)*,[15] given to a number of persons by the king.[15a]

---

[13] Cf. UT, p. 460, No. 1907; the translation of *Ch. Virolleaud*, PRU, V, p. 40, by comparison with Hbr. *ᶜaqōb* "hill-country," is unconvincing. Here we have a verbal, not a noun form; cf. Hebr. *piᶜel* of *ᶜqb*, "to delay," "to retard," and in connectinon with it, possibly the Ugaritic "to be located." Cf. also *M. Dietrich, O. Loretz*, Zur ugaritischen Lexicographie, I, BiOr, 23, 1966, p. 131.

[14] The last line of the text, 10, gives *šd Ṯbᶜm [. . .]y*, "The field of *Ṯbᶜm* man of (?) . . ."; the last letter *y* could be the ending of a nisb, and therefore it is possible that an additional place-name was mentioned here.

[15] *ubdy*, cf. a) *Rainey*, Social Structure, p. 32, 120–21, a fief connected with service and natural payments. *A. F. Rainey* agrees also that the word is of Hittite origin; b) *H. G. Güterbock*, "Oriens," X, 1957, p. 36, explains the term by the Hittite *upatiya;* c) *G. Rinaldi*, Osservazioni sugli elenchi ugaritici *šd ubdy*, *ubdy*, Melanges E. Tisserant, I, Vaticano, 1964, pp. 345–49, *ubdy*, "occupied," or "delivered into disposal," (field-*šd*); d) UT, p. 349, No. 17, "perpetual land grant," but the explanation of *C. H. Gordon* is unconvincing. The explanations of *Güterbock* and *Rinaldi* are not in contradiction, but one aids the other in understanding the true meaning of the term.

[15a] Cf. also ZUL, VII UF, V, 1975, p. 94, No. 6, where the text is partially discussed.

1) *spr. ubdy. Art*	"1) List of holdings (from the king in the village) *Art*.
2) *šd. Prn. bd. Agpṯn nḥlh*	2) The field of *Prn* to (lit. "into the hands") *Agpṯn* (and) his descendents.
3) *šd. S_2wn bd. Ttyn. nḥ[lh]*	3) The field of *S_2wn* to *Ttyn* (and) his descendents.
4) *šd Tṯyn. [b]n. Arkš[x].* 5) *l[]q[. . .]*	4) The field of *Tṯyn*. [s]on of *Arkš[ ]* 5) to . . .[16]
6) *šd. []l. bd. qrt*	6) The field of [x]. to the village[17]
7) *šd. Ann[ḏ]r. bd. Bdn.[.]nḥ[lh]*	7) The field of *Ann[ḏ]r*, to *Bdn* (and) [his] descenden[ts].
8) *[šd.] Gyn. bd. Kmrm. n[ḥl]h*	8) [The field] of *Gyn* to *Kmrm* (and) his descenden[ts].
9) *[š]d. Nbzn. []l.qrt*	9) the [fie]ld of *Nbzn* [] to the village.[17]
10) *[š]d. Agpṯr. bd. Sḫrn. nḥlh*	10) The [fi]eld of *Agptr* to *Sḫrn* (and) his descendents.
11) *šd. Annmn. bd. Tyn. nḥlh*	11) The field of *Annmn* to *Tyn* (and) his descendents.
12) *šd. Pġyn [b]d. []r[]n. l. Ty⟨n⟩ [n]ḥlh.*	12) The field of *Pġyn* [t]o [. .]r [. .]n to *Tyn* (and) his [des]cendents.
13) *šd. Krz. bn. Ann. ᶜ[] . . .*	13) The field of *Krz*. son of *Ann* . . .
14) *šd. Ṯ[r]yn. bn. Tkn. bd. qrt.*	14) The field of *Ṯ[r]yn*. son of *Tkn* to the village[17]
15) *šd[]. dyn bd. Pln. nḥlh*	15) The field of . . . *dyn* to *Pln* (and) his heirs.
16) *šd. Irdyn. bn. Ḫrġš[]. l. qrt*	16) The field of *Irdyn*, son of *Ḫrġš* [ ] to the village.
17) *šd. Iġlyn. bn. Krzbn. l. qrt*	17) The field of *Iġlyn*, son of *Krzbn* to the village.[17]
18) *šd. Pln. bn. Tiyn. bd[.] Ilmhr nḥlh*	18) The field of *Pln*, son of *Tiyn*, to *Ilmhr* (and) his descendents.

[16] Reconstruction based on the autography uncertain.

[17] Or the *âlu*-village *Qrt*, known from PRU, II, 24 (UT, 1024); PRU, V, 44 (UT, 2044); 118 (UT, 2118, etc.). The fact that the fields are located in the village *Art* seems to prove that the word *qrt* has to be translated here as "village." But even if it is the village *Qrt* our conclusions are unchanged.

19) *šd Knn [.] bd. Ann. ᶜdb*	19) The field of *Knn* to *Annᶜdb*[18]
20) *šd Il[xx]. bn Ir[x]ṯr. l. Sḫrn nḥlh*	20) The field of *Il[xx]*, son of *Ir[x]ṯr*, to *Sḫrn* (and) his heirs
21) *šd [x]pṯn. b[n]*[19] *Brrn. l. qrt*	21) The field of *[ ]pṯn*, son[19] of *Brrn*, to the village[17]
22) *šd [x]dy. bn[.] Brzn*	22) The field of *[ ]dy*, son of *Brzn*,
23) *l. qrt.*	23) to the village."

There are twenty-one fields listed in the text. In most cases "the field of "x" (personal name)" is handed over to another person, "y." Sometimes "his descendents" *(nḥlh)* are also mentioned. This text is typical of those tablets found in the archives of Ugarit, which dealt with the redistribution of the royal landfund to people in the royal service. The lands were confiscated from certain persons, perhaps *nayyālu*. (Cf. above, Ch. IV, p. 57.) But lines 6, 9, 14, 16, 21, and 22–23, indicate that six fields were not distributed to individuals, but were given to one village—*Art*. It is not clear if the rural community received the fields as their property, or only for temporary holding. Were these lands considered part of the landfund, where the villagers had to work collectively for the treasury, delivering to it the products of their labor ? Or were the fields distributed to certain individuals or families inside the community ? It is most likely that these lands remained royal property and served the purposes of distribution and redistribution. It is obvious that the royal administration had dealings with these people. Even when they continued to be members of the rural community, the land remained royal. Still, the rural community, through its local administration, or individual who were in charge of the village *(qrt)*, managed the fields. If the land were distributed to individuals inside the community it is more likely that "*l qrt*" would not have been written in the text. Thus, it is more realistic to suppose that the communal authorities dealt with the fields and their management. It is also possible that the crops harvested from these fields had to be paid to the treasury. This was, therefore, an additional tax imposed on the village *Art*.

In referring to the *eqlāt*ᴹ *ṣi-ib-bi-ru* ("the *ṣibbiru* fields"), we may suppose that this type of land was similar to "public lands" (ager publi-

---

[18] The word-dividing sign may be a result of scribal error, but cf. also ZUL, VII, UF, V, p. 94, No. 60.

[19] *Gordon*, UT, *b[d]*, but such a reconstruction is impossible, for we have *l qrt*, "to the village." Thus, *b[n]* is a more logical reconstruction and also in accordance with other similar lines of the same text.

cus), but in this case the lands were only under royal disposition. However, additional data concerning this situation is highly questionable.

According to PRU, III, 16.137, King *Niqmaddu* II took land in various places, among them 7) *eqlāt ṣi-ib-bi-ri* 8) *i-na* narRa-aḫ-ba-ni, "the *ṣibbiru* fields in (the region) of (the river) *Raḫbanu.*" He handed them over to his *maryannu*[20] and *mūdu*[21] serviceman, *Abdu*, son of *Abdinergal*. According to PRU, III, 16.233, this same person received one *eqil ṣi-ib-bi-ri ("ṣibbiru field")*. This term also appears in the large but fragmentary text, PRU, VI, 55 (RS. 18.22). We do not know all of the conditions by which the king handed over, or withdrew, the fields. The text mentions at least 1(?), 1(?), 4(?), 2, 7, 20, and 25 fields which were at the disposal of certain persons of certain persons of the village *Riqdu (amēl Riq-di)*.[22] They were all defined as *ša i-na eqlāt*M *ṣi-ib-bi-ri* ("which lay among (or "are of") the *ṣibbiru* fields." How these fields were dealt with further is unclear.

We lack a clear understanding of the term *ṣibbiru*. The translation of J. Nougayrol "territoire collectif" or "territoire du travail collectif" ("collective territory" or "territory for collective work")[23] is given without any further explanation. Perhaps J. Nougayrol had in mind the Hebrew-Mishnaitic *ṣibbūr* ("community") or the Ugaritic *ṣbr*, which appears in the same sense in some passages in Ugaritic mythologic texts.[24] In our own opinion, the *ṣibbiru*, occurring in the non-legendary texts mentioned above, is closely related to PRU, V, 73 (UT. 2073).

1) *ṯn. ṣbrm*	"1) Two (fields) *ṣbr*
2) *b. Uškn*	2) in (the village) *Uškn*
3) *ṣbr ḥd*	3) One *ṣbr* (field)
4) *b. Ar*	4) in (the village) *Ar*
5) *ṣbr. aḥd.*	5) One *ṣbr* (field)
6) *b. Mlk*	6) In (the village) *Mlk*
7) *ṣbr. aḥd*	7) One *ṣbr* (field)
8) b. *Mʿrby*	8) In (the village) *Mʿrby*

[20] On the role and position of the *maryannu*-servicemen-chariot-warriors in Ugarit, cf. *Heltzer*, Soziale Aspekte, pp. 125–29, and OAC, IX, 1969.

[21] On the *mūdu* servicemen in Ugarit, cf. *M. Heltzer*, Ugaritic-Akkadian Etymologies *(mūdu/md(m))*, SY, II_1, 1965, pp. 355–58.

[22] Only one man, I*I-ru-na*, was a "man of Ugarit" *(amêl* al*U-ga-ri-it)*.

[23] PRU, VI, p. 146.

[24] UT, p. 472, No. 2142; cf. below, Ch. VI, pp. 76–77, cf. also, CAD, 16, p. 203, where *ṣippiri* is explained as "a type of field," and the word, occurring in Akkadian from Ugarit, is defined as a "West-Semitic word," at the same time. CAD, 16, p. 202, *ṣipirtu*, is given also as occurring in Middle-Babylonian, *ultu ṣi-pi-ir-ti adi namgar*, "from the *ṣipirtu* to the irrigation ditch." The word occurs only once, and in our opinion it has to be read *ṣibirtu* in Babylonian and Ugaritic texts.

9) *ṣbr. aḥd*	9) One *ṣbr* (field)
10) *b. Ulm*	10) in (the village) *Ulm*
11) *ṣbr aḥd*	11) One *ṣbr* (field)
12) *b. Ubr^{c}y*	12) in (the village) *Ubr^{c}y*."

It seems that this text is also referring to the *ṣibbiru* fields quoted from the tablets in Akkadian,[25] although in the village of *Riqdi* there were at least sixty units, and here we have two only in *Uškn*, and one in each of the other villages (*Ar*, *Mlk*, *M^{c}rby*, *Ulm*, and *Ubr^{c}y*). It seems that the *ṣibbiru (ṣbr?)* fields were bound to some administrative procedure by the authorities of Ugarit. Perhaps they were collectively worked by the villagers.[26] The term by itself seems to allude to this. But the question is not definitively answered. It is clear, as we have seen, that there were certain categories of lands which were managed by the village. This offers an additional proof of the communal character of the village.

Local Religious Cults and Communal (Local) Sanctuaries in the Kingdom of Ugarit

Naturally, the villages of the kingdom had to participate in the religious cults of the whole country and, as we have seen from text PRU, V, 4 (UT. 2004), the villages had to deliver certain quantities of wine for royal sacrifices.[27] Still, a certain number of villages had their own cults, or were attached to some special religious cults. It is clear, that some of the villages had theoforic names. We know, for instance, of the villages of ^{al}*Beqa-*^{il}*Ištar*, "Valley of (the goddess) *Ištar* or *Aštart*;" *Ilštm^{c}*; *Mril*;[28] *Mati-ilu*; *Šlmy*;[29] ^{al}*Ašri-*^{il}*Ba'ala*;[30] *Ḫb/pty* (Akk. *Ḫu-up-pa-tu*);[31] *Qdš* (Akk. *Qidšu*);[32]

[25] Cf. UT, p. 472, No. 2142. *ṣbr-*" a team (of workers)" in this context; cf. also *M. Dietrich*, *O. Loretz*, Zur ugaritischen Lexikographie, I, BiOr, 23, 1966, p. 132, where *ṣbr* in PRU, V, 73 is compared with Old-Assyrian *ṣupru*, "seized debtor"; both explanations are unacceptable; a more detailed discussion of this issue, cf. *M. Heltzer*, Die *ṣibbiru-Felder* in Ugarit, to be published in "Orientalia Lovainensis Periodica."

[26] Thus I must abandon my former explanation of the term *ṣbr* as meaning "assembly (of the people) of the village," *M. Heltzer*, Aspects of Social History, p. 37.

[27] Cf. above, Ch. II, pp. 40–41.

[28] In Akkadian texts *il* = *ilu* ("god"), in these place-names.

[29] The Ugaritic pantheon knows the god *Šlm*, cf. UT, p. 490, No. 2424.

[30] The "place", "site", *ašru*, of the god *B^{c}l*.

[31] The place-name composed by the name of the Hurrian goddess, *Ḫeb/pa(t)*.

[32] The deity *Qadeš*, "The Holy one," broadly known as a Canaanite god or goddess.

Ḫlb Ṣpn (Akk. *Ḫalbu* ḫuršan*Ḫa-zi*).[33] The names of other deities did not coincide with the names of the villages where they were worshipped, for example, *Ḫebat* of (the village) *Ari*.[34] The cult of *Rešef* is known from PRU, II, 154 (UT, 1154), and was worshipped in the village of *Ilštm*ᶜ. This problem brings us to text CTC, 31 (UT, 14).

1) *bt. Il* 2) *b*ᶜ*l. bt. Aḏmny* 3) *b*ᶜ*l. bt. Pdy* 4) *b*ᶜ*l. bt. Nqly* 5) *b*ᶜ*l. bt.* ᶜ*lr* 6) *b*ᶜ*l. bt. Ssl* 7) *b*ᶜ*l. bt. Ṯrn* 8) *b*ᶜ*l. bt. Ktmn* 9) *[b*ᶜ*]l. bt. Ndbd* 10) *[b*ᶜ*l. bt.] Ṣnr* 11) *[b*ᶜ*l]. bt. Bsn*.[35]

"1) Sanctuary[36] of *Il*,[37] 2) lord of the temple (sanctuary) of *Aḏmn*,[38] 3) lord of the temple of the village *Pd(y)*,[39] 4) lord of the temple *Nqly*, 5) lord of the temple of ᶜ*lr*, 6) lord of the temple of *Ssl*, 7) lord of the temple of *Ṯrn*, 8) lord of the temple of *Ktmn*, 9) [lo]rd of the sanctuary of *Addu* in (the village) *Ndb*,[40] 10) [lord of the temple] of (the village) *Ṣnr*,[41] 11) [lord] of the temple of *Bsn*."

This text came from the temple-archives, where religious and mythological, but almost no administrative texts were held. Therefore, it is impossible to agree with those scholars who find in this tablet a patronymic list, as Yankovskaya and other scholars propose.[42] In our opinion it contains a list of sanctuaries (probably incomplete) subdued to the god Il, head of the Ugaritic pantheon. Among the ten names given, Eshmoun and *Addu* (Adad) are the names of highly venerated gods in Ugarit. Five names, ᶜ*lr*, *Ssl*, *Ṯrn*, *Ktmn*, and *Bsn*, are completely lacking in other texts. Only *Pdy*, *Ṣnr* and *Ndb(y)* are the names of Ugaritic villages. It seems to be clear that all these local sanctuaries, named according to the place-

---

33 Connected with the Ugaritic and Canaanite deity *Ṣaphon;* cf. *W. F. Albright*, Baal-Zephon, "Festschrift für A. Bertholet," Tübingen, 1950, pp. 4–14. The worship of this deity in Ugarit was connected with the holy mountain, *Ṣafōn* (Akk. *Ḫazi*, Classical *Mons Casius*).

34 PRU, IV, 17.369B, 1, v'5'8'—il*Ḫe-bat* al*A-ri*.

35 Cf. the discussion on this text: *N. B. Yankovskaya*, L'autonomie de la communauté á Ugarit, VDI, 1963, No. 3, p. 39 (Russian); *M. Heltzer*, Once More on Communal Self-Government in Ugarit, VDI, 1965, No. 2, p. 7 (Russian); cf. ZUL, XI, UF, VI, 1974, p. 22, No. 20.

36 *bt*, lit. "house," has often had the meaning "sanctuary" in all Semitic languages, but this is especially the case in Ugaritic.

37 Principal deity of the Ugaritic pantheon.

38 The god *Eshmoun*, Phoen. *'šmn*.

39 al*Pidi/Pd(y)*, U, V, 12 (RS. 17.150); PRU, V, 27, 8 (UT, 2027); 42, 3 (UT, 2042.3); 112, 2 (UT, 242,2), and many other texts.

40 From *Ndb* + *hd*, cf. WUS, p. 202, No. 1752; *Ndby* as a place-name, cf. PRU, IV, 17.62, 17; 17.339A—al*Ni-da-bi*, PRU, V, 119, 13–15.

41 al*S/Zi-na-ru/Snr*—cf. CTC, 71, 33 (UT, 113); PRU, II, 84, 14 (UT, 1084); PRU, III, 11.800; PRU, V, 41, 8 (UT, 2041), etc.

name or deity, or both (*Ndbd*, cf. above), were located in various places of the kingdom of Ugarit.

It is natural that the local cults also had their priests, or at least people who were in charge. One such person was "*Milkiyatanu*, son of *Mi[. . .]*, priest of Ba'al (of the village) [ ]," (*^{I}Mil-ki-yatānu, mâr ki[. . .]* ^{amel}*šangu ša* ^{il}Ba-'-li ^{al}*[. . .]*).[43]

In another case, a certain *Ṣtqn* is mentioned in PRU, II, 154 (UT, 1144), in relation to the sacrifices in the local community. This passage, which is of interest to us, follows.

4) *gdy lqḥ Ṣtqn g(?)t*[44] *bn ndr* 5) *umr [ ]tn ṯṯ ḫsn lytn* 6) *lrḥ [ ]t(?) lqḥ Ṣtqn* 7) *bt qbṣ ur[ ]t Ilštm*^{c} *dbḥ Ṣtqn l* 8) *Ršp.*

"4) *Ṣtqn* takes a lamb which (?) is (of the man) who gave his vow(?)[45] 5) He looks(?)[46] . . . six *ḫsn*[47] for to give. 6) To his hand[48] *Ṣtqn* takes, 7) (in) the assembly[49] house, . . . of (the village) *Ilštm*^{c} *Ṣtqn* sacrifices to 9) (the god) *Ršp.*"

We see that the village *Ilštm*^{c}, well-known from various sources, also had its cult of the god Reshef, one of the gods of the Ugaritic pantheon. It is interesting that *Ilštm*^{c} had its own *bt qbṣ* ("assembly house"). The fact that the sacrifice ceremony was communal gives additional evidence of the communal character of the village. Although we have no parallel texts which mention the *bt qbṣ*, it may be comparable to the *bt ḫbr* in the epic of King Keret.[50]

---

[42] *Yankovskaya*, L'autonomie, pp. 39–40; all references given in ZUL, XI, UF, VII, 1974, p. 22.

[43] *Ch. Virolleaud*, Cinq tablettes accadiennes de Ras Shamra, RA, XXXVII, 1940, No. 1, text II.

[44] The autograph of this word is unclear, and the transcription is according to *Virolleaud*, PRU, II, p. 184, and *C. Gordon*, UT. The text itself was written running around the tablet, so that each line is formed by reading the obverse and reverse, the *y(?)t* stands on the edge. Possibly, *dt* was the original word, in which case we must translate it as "which."

[45] Literally, "son of the vow."

[46] *umr*, cf. UT, p. 361, No. 229 *'mr*, "to look," "to see," WUS, p. 25, No. 283. *W. Leslau*, Observations on Semitic Cognates in Ugaritic, Or., 32, 1968, p. 349, gives the ethiopic *'a'mara* "know," "recognize."

[47] Perhaps the plural st. cstr, but the meaning of the word is unclear. It does not seem to be a personal name, or a certain professional, as the dictionaries explain; WUS, p. 114, No. 1056–59; UT, p. 403, No. 985.

[48] *rḥt*, "hand," cf. Arab. *rāḥat(un)*, Akk. *rittu*.

[49] *qbṣ*—Hebrew, *q*^{e}*būṣā*, "gathering, assembly," the *bt qbṣ* is not known from other texts.

[50] I Krt (CTC, 14 = UT, Krt): 80) ^{c}*db akl lqryt* 81) *ḥtt lbt ḫbr* ("He prepared bread for the city 81) wheat for the *ḫbr*-house"). *ḫbr* may be "gathering, fellow, company," etc.

All of the above indicates beyond doubt that communal local religious cults really existed in Ugarit.

After studying various communal features in the kingdom of Ugarit, we come to the question of local communal self-government. This will be discussed in Chapter VI.

CHAPTER VI

COMMUNAL SELF-GOVERNMENT IN THE VILLAGES AND ITS RELATION TO THE ROYAL ADMINISTRATION

Types of Local Self-government According to Various Non-administrative Sources

In the mythological and epical texts from Ugarit, which were composed some centuries before they were written down (XIV–XIII centuries b.c.), the word *pḫr* (var. *pḫyr*) meant "assembly," designating the "assembly of the gods" *(pḫr ilm)*, or "assembly of the sons of *Il (mpḫrt bn Il)*.[1] Although this word does not occur in the administrative texts of the fourteenth to thirteenth centuries, it helps us understand the general direction of the political ideology of Ugarit. Royal rule did not exclude the possibilities of assemblies and other representative bodies.[2]

As was mentioned above,[3] text PRU, II, 154 mentions the "assembly house" or "house of the gathering" *(bt qbṣ)* of the village of *Ilštm*ᶜ. Also discussed was the *bt ḫbr* in the Keret epic. The same epic offers a parallel concerning tribal or communal or some other type cf assemblies. CTC, 15, III (UT, 128): 13) *mid rm Krt* 14) *btk rpi arṣ* 15) *bpḫr qbṣ. dtn* ("13) Arise much, O Keret! 14) among the heroes(?)[4] of the country // 15) in the gathered assembly of *dtn*".[5]

The Ugaritic epic of Danel contains a reference to some kind of local assembly also. The text, II Dnil V (= UT. 2 Aqht), relates that 6) *(Dnil) yṯb. bap. tǵr. tḥt* 7) *adrm. dbgrn. ydn* 8) *dn. almnt. yṯpṭ. ṯpṭ. ytm.* ("6) (Danel) sits in front of the gate // under (among) 7) the nobles,[6] who are on the

---

[1] WUS, pp. 255, No. 2215; UT. p. 468, No. 2037; cf. *W. Leslau*, Observations on Semitic Cognates in Ugaritic, Or., 37, 1968, p. 361.

[2] Cf. *Th. Jacobsen*, Early Political Development in Mesopotamia, ZA, 18 (52), 1957, pp. 91–140; *I. M. Diakonoff*, Society and State in Ancient Mesopotamia, Moscow, 1959, (Russian with English summary).

[3] Chapter V, p. 73.

[4] Cf. WUS, p. 295, No. 2527; UT, p. 485, No. 2346. Cf. also, a controversial opinion, *J. C. de Moor*, UF, 1969, I, p. 176, "The Healer" (without translation); *S. B. Parker*, UF, II, 1970, p. 243.

[5] WUS, p. 83, No. 801, "lord"; UT, No. 712, tribal name. It is more likely that this name is the name of a deity or a hero, cf. U, V, No. 6 (Ugar, RS. 24.272), 1) *k ymǵy. adn.* 2) *ilm. rmb.* ᶜ*m dtn* 3) *w. yšal. mtpṭ yld* ("1) When the lord 2) of the great gods arrives to *Dtn* 3) and asks the judgement about the child").

[6] *adrm*—"nobles," cf. *aṯt adrt* ("noble wife"), and PRU, II, 92 (UT, 1092), 6) *arb*ᶜ *yn[. . .]* 7) *b. adrm [ ]* 8) *šqym.* ("6) 4 (jare) of wine [ ] 7) for the nobles (elders ?)

threshing-floor,[7] he decides 8) in the case of the widow, judges the judgment of the orphan").

This text illustrates various traditions of primitive democracy as shown also in the other literary texts of Ugarit. Besides the epical texts, as in the case of the "assembly of the gods" (cf. above), various terms of the "primitive democracy" appear also in the purely mythological poems. The expression which is of interest to us appears four times in the known texts in almost the same wording. CTC, 6 (UT, 49 and 62) deals with the death of the god Aliyan Ba'al and the joy of his enemies on this event. 11) . . . *tšmḫ ht* 12) *Aṯrt. wbnh. Ilt wṣb* 13) *rt. aryh, kmt Aliyn* 14) *Bᶜl. kḫlq. zbl. bᶜl* 15) *arṣ*[8] . . .

"11) . . . there will rejoice 12) *Aširat* and her sons,
Ilat[9] and the *ṣbrt* 13) of her *ary's*.
Because dead is *Aliyan* 14) *Baal*
Because the noble, lord of the earth perished."[10]

The same expression occurs in a slightly different form in CTC, 4 (UT, 51), II, where the text is partly destroyed. 25) . . . *ṣ]brt* 26) *aryy [. . .]*. We seem to have here the plural form with the possessive pronominal suffix of the first person singular. Thus, the meaning is: "the *ṣbrt* of my *ary's*." Following the rules of the poetic structure of the text, which employs the parallelismus membrorum, we see that *aryh* has its parallel meaning in *bnh*, "here sons." The Danel epic employs *aryh* in parallelism with *aḫh* "his brothers."[11] This contributes to the understanding of the real meaning of the word *ary*, "kinsman."[12] Taking into account all the above, it is

---

[] 8) who give to drink"), perhaps the literally translation has to be "mighty" (cf. Hebr. *'addir*); cf. WUS, p. 8, No. 95; UT, p. 352, No. 92.

[7] *grn*—"threshing floor" as place for assemblies and trials in front of the gate, cf. *S. Smith*, On the Meaning of Goren, PEQ, 85, 1953, pp. 42–45; *J. Gray*, The Goren of the City Gate, PEQ, 85, 1953, pp. 118–23; WUS, p. 69, No. 699; UT, p. 381, No. 622; *Leslau*, Observations, p. 352.

[8] Cf. the translation, *J. Aistleitner*, Die Mythologischen und Kultischen Texte aus Ras Schamra, Budapest, 1959, pp. 18–19.

[9] Or simply, "the goddess."

[10] The same wording cf. *(Aṯrt w bnh Ilt w ṣbrt aryh)*, CTC, 4, IV, 49–50 (UT, 51); CTC, 3 (UT, ᶜ*nt*), V, 45.

[11] CTC, 17 (UT, 2 *Aqht*), I, 19; 19) *din. bn. lh* 20) *km. aḫh. w. šrš. km. aryh* 21) *bl. iṯ. bn. lh. km. aḫh. wšrš* 22) *km. aryh* ("19) for he has no son 20) like his brothers, and (no) offspring like his *ary(s)* 21) he has no son, like his brothers, and offspring 22) like his *ary(s)*"). II, 14) . . . *kyld. bn. ly. km* 15) *aḫy. wšrš. km aryy* ("14) . . . when a son shall be born to me like 15) to my brothers, and an offspring like to my *ary's*").

[12] WUS, p. 35, No. 3021; UT, p. 366, No. 349. The only linguistic parallel given here is Eg. *iry*, "companion."

impossible to agree with the translation of *ṣbrt* as "mob"[13] or "band, group."[14] In our opinion, we are dealing with a more precisely defined social term. We must, therefore, base ourselves on the meaning of the root *ṣbr* in Hebrew, "to gather, to bring together," as well as the Mishnaitic meaning of *ṣibbūr*, "assembly, community."[15] Although in Ugaritic the word appears in the feminine form, it must have had nearly the same meaning, i.e., "entity," "assembly," "community." Thus, the mythological passage has to be translated, "*Aširat* and her sons // *Ilat* and the community of her kinsmen."

We have analyzed above the terms concerning the origins of communal self-government, as found in archaic mythological and epical texts. We may now use these terms as an aid to understanding similar terms found in texts of greater historical reliability.

Communal Assemblies

Although we have no direct mention of communal assemblies in Ugarit, the mere fact that the communities had to bear collective responsibility (cf. above, Ch. V, pp. 63–65), and possessed a *bt qbṣ*, "house of assembly" (cf. above, Ch. V, pp. 73–74), enables us to draw the conclusion that such institutions existed. Some of the available documents shed additional light on this issue, e.g., PRU, V, 116 (UT, 2116).[16]

1) *Tldn* 2) *Ṯrkn* 3) *Kli* 4) *Plǵn* 5) *Aps*$_2$*ny* 6) *ᶜrb[. . .]n [xxx]*[16a] 7) *w.b. p[n]*[17] 8) *Aps*$_2$*[nyy]*[18] 9) *b. yṣih[m]* 10) *ḥwt[. .]*[18a] 11) *alp k[sp]* 12) *ts*$_2$*ᶜn[hm](?)*[19] 13) *w. hm. al[p]*[20] 14) *l. ts*$_2$*ᶜn* 15) *Mṣrm* 16) *tmkrn* 17) *ypḥ.*

---

[13] WUS, p. 263, No. 2301.

[14] UT, p. 472, No. 2142.

[15] Cf. *Levy*, IV, p. 164, Aram. *ṣibbūrā*, with the same meaning; cf. also, Ch. V, pp. 70–74 about the *ṣbr* in various villages.

[16] *M. Liverani*, Due documenti con garantia di presenza, U, VI, P. 1969, pp. 375–78; *M. Dietrich, O. Loretz, J. Sanmartín*, Keilalphabetische Bürgschaftsdokumente aus Ugarit, UF, VI, pp. 466–67.

[16a] According to UF, VI.

[17] The autograph enables us to read the remnants of the two letters, which were not taken into account by *Ch. Virolleaud*.

[18] *Ch. Virolleaud* reconstructed this as *Aps*$_2$*[ny]*, but the space demands three signs.

[18a] The reconstructions of Liverani and UF, VI *[ṯth]* and *[ṯthm]* are unacceptable.

[19] Our reconstruction; space for 1–2 signs.

[20] Our reconstruction; the remains of the sign p are legible on an autograph.

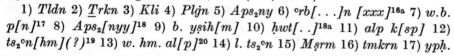

ᶜbdilt 18) *bn. M.* 19) *ypḥ Ilšlm* 20) *bn. Prqdš* 21) *ypḥ Mnḥm* 22) *bn. Ḫnn* 23) *Brqn spr.*

"1) *Tldn,* 2) *Ṯrkn,* 3) *Kli* (and) 4) *Plǵn*—5) people of (the village) *Apsn (Apsuna)* 6) took [on themselves mutual] guaranties.[21] 7) And in the [presence] 8) [of the people] of *Apsuna* 9) at their departure[22] 10) (by) their lives [they have sworn][23] 11) about (1) thousand (sheqels of) sil[ver] 12) for [their] travel. 13) And they have thou[sand] 14) for (their) travel 15) to Egypt 16) for their *tamkar* operations. 17) Witness[24] *ᶜbdilt,* 18) son of *M;*[25] 19) witness *Ilšlm,* 20) son of *Prqdš;* 21) witness *Mnḥm,* 22) son of *Ḫnn.* 23) *Brqn,* the scribe."

In our opinion this text is unique among the alphabetic documents available from Ugarit at present. It is a contract of "comradeship," or "companionship"—*tappūtu,* known also from various Mesopotamian sources.[26] Four people combined their resources for a commercial expedition to Egypt. In our case, the most important thing is that the text has witnesses. Despite this, the transaction was also made in the presence of the people of *Apsuna,* the native village of the four. Thus, there was a gathering or assembly of the people of the village, who also make legal confirmation of the document. Otherwise, the people of *Apsuna* would not have been mentioned. Unfortunately, there is no additional information available concerning an assembly of the people of a village.

We also know of one case in which people of a certain village had treaty relations with the royal authorities. The small text, PRU, II 173 (UT, 1173), relates: 1) *mṣmt ᶜbs* 2) *arr. d. ǵr* 3) *ht.*[26a] "1) Treaty[27] (of) *ᶜbs* "with" or "of"[27a] 2) *Arr*[28] (of) (or "about") the mountain(?) 3) Ht."[28a] But un-

---

[21] *ᶜrb,* "to enter," also, "to guarantee"; cf. Akk. *erēbu* and Hebr. *ᶜrb.*

[22] I.e., at the departure of the four participants of the agreement, who gave the mutual guaranties.

[23] UT, p. 395, No. 850, "house, dynasty, realm," is completely obscure in this case; the word is connected with *ḥyy/ḥwy,* cf. No. 856; *M. Liverani,* pp. 375–78, gives a different interpretation of this text. He compares the tablet with PRU, II, 161 (UT. 1161); *ᶜrb b* he interprets as "to grant," 10) *hwt [ṯth]* ("la vita (dei garanti) e la sua (del debitore sostituta").

[24] UT, p. 412, No. 1129.

[25] This is the way it appears in the text; our article "Ein ugaritischer Genossenschaftsvertrag" will be published elsewhere.

[26] CH § 99; *A. Finet,* Le code de Hammurapi, Paris, 1973, pp. 71–72, etc.

[26a] According to the revised reading in ZUL, VII, p. 100, No. 72.

[27] *Dietrich, Loretz,* Der Vertrag, p. 218, proves the identity of the Akk. *rikiltu* with Ug. *mṣmt,* "treaty, contract."

[27a] Personal name(?).

[28] ZUL, VII, p. 100—"*ᶜbs* (from) *Arr,*" but such an abridged form on a small etiquet can also denote that the treaty was concluded with the village *Arr.*

[28a] Cf. ZUL, VII.

fortunately, there is no additional information and, except for the fact that there existed some cases of treaty relations between the villages and the authorities or individuals, it is impossible to draw any conclusions.

The Council of Elders

We possess very little data concerning councils of elders. A certain institution of "fathers *(*^{amel}*abbē*^{M}*)* existed in Ugarit. In text PRU, IV, 17. 424C, *Addudayyānu*, king of *Amqi*, complies with an illegal demand, made by the *sākinu* (vizier) of Ugarit, for customs duties imposed on his trade agent or *tamkar*. . . . 24) . . . *ša-'a-al* 25) $^{\text{[ame]l}}$*abbē*^{M} ^{al}*Ú-ga-ri-it* 26) *[ki-i] il-qa-a mik-[*sa*]* 27) *[iš]-tu qâti*^{ti} ^{amel}*tam[kāri ša šêpi-šu(?)].*[29] "24) . . . Ask 25) the "fathers" of Ugarit 26) [did] (somebody) take custom [duties] 27) from the *tam[kar]* [of his feet] (personal *tamkar*)."[30] The term "fathers" seems to refer to a collective body, perhaps composed of elders, which preserved some kind of oral legal tradition. But, there is no proof that this body existed in the villages of the kingdom of Ugarit.

More precise data is gained from U, V, 52 (RS. 20.239). From this text, we learn that in a certain legal case the elders of the *âlu Rakba* had to enter the sanctuary and to give an oath. The council of elders consisted of *Babiyanu*, son of *Yadudana; Abdu* and his son (or sons); *Addunu*, his son-in-law; and the "head of thousand (men)" *(*^{amel}*akil li-im).*[31] The council thus consisted of at least five persons. But these elders *(*^{amelM}*šî-būtu*^{M}*)* by no means comprised a democratic institution. First of all, we see that at least three persons (*Abdu*, his sor, and son-in-law) were close relatives. One of the elders *(akil li-im)* was a man of high rank in the royal administration. Perhaps he was also a landowner inside the rural community. But the characteristic feature is that the eldership was distributed among members of one family, and high-ranking officials. It is possible that the councils of elders of the other villages were of a similar nature, although we have almost no additional information on this subject.[32]

---

[29] Reconstructed by *J. Nougayrol*, based on similar passages in the same text.

[30] Translation of *ša šêpē-šu*—"personal," cf. *M. Heltzer*, The *tamkar* and His Role, pp. 9–10; cf. also, PRU, IV, 205, 10, ^{amel}*abu*, in a fragmentary text.

[31] For the full text and translation see Ch. V, pp. 64–65.

[32] Cf. also the broken text U, V, 66 (RS. 21.54B) which relates: 1) *[*^{amelM}$_{2}$*šîb]ūtu*^{M} 2) *[ša* ^{al}*A]r-ru-ti* 3) *[i-na eka]lli-ka an-na-kum* ("[The el]ders 2) [of the (village) *A*]*rutu*, 3) [who in] this your [pal]ace"), 4) *[lu-u (?) i]t-ta-mu* ("[must give] the oath"). On the council of elders in related ancient oriental societies, cf. *J. L. McKen-*

Heads of the Local Administration and Their Relationship to the Royal Authorities

The terms used to designate people in high positions in the village administration are not clearly defined. As we will show below, the words *ḫazannu, sākinu/skn, rb*, and others, could be used for designating royal officials of high rank, appointed to carry out certain functions in the whole kingdom, as well as local officials, and even representatives of the local self-government. Therefore, we have to investigate every individual case and deal with this question very carefully.

1. *Ḫazannu.* In various villages of the kingdom, people who received landholdings from the king, and who possessed certain privileges because they were also in the royal service, were freed from administrative power of the "*ḫazannu* of the village." PRU, III, 15.137, from the period of *Amistamru* II, referring to a certain *Abdiḫagab*, a "royal friend" *(mūdu šarri)*, tells us: 13) *ù* amel*ḫa-za-nu âli*KI *ù* amel*akil e[q]lāti*M 14) *la-a i-ma-li-ik eli-šu.* "13) And the *ḫazannu* of the village, and the overseer of the f[iel]ds 14) shall not have power over him." We must draw the conclusion that there was a *ḫazannu* in every village, and unlike those having special privileges, he had some power over the main mass of the local population, the peasants of the rural community.[33]

The situation is more complicated in U, V, 26 (RS. 20.03) where a Hittite prince or royal official, *Šukurtešub*, wrote to king *Ammistamru* II of Ugarit:

14) *[i]-na-an-na a-nu-um-ma* 15) [am]elM*ṣa-ri-pu-tu* 16) *mârē* al*Pa-ni-iš-ta-'a* 17) *a-na muḫ-ḫi-ka al-ta-pár* 18) *máš-da-a-ri a-na e-pé-ši* 19) *i-na*

zie, The Elders in the Old Testament, AB, 10, Rome, 1959, pp. 388–406; *D. A. McKenzie*, Judicial Procedure at the Town Gate, VT, XIV, 1964, No. 1, pp. 100–104; *P. Artzi*, "*Vox populi*" in the Amarna Tablets, RA, 1964, No. 4, pp. 159–66; *J. A. Wilson*, The Assembly of a Phoenician City, JNES, IV, 1945, No. 4, p. 245; *H. Klengel*, Die Rolle der Ältesten *[LÚ*MEŠ *ŠU. GI]* in Kleinasien der Hethiterzeit, ZA, 23 (57), 1965, pp. 223–36; *H. Klengel*, Zu den *šībūtum* in Altbabylonischer Zeit, Or., 29, 1969, No. 4, pp. 357–75; *H. Reviv*, On Urban Representative Institutions and Self-Government in Syria-Palestine, JESHO, XII, 1969, pp. 283–97; *M. Liverani*, Communantés . . ., JESHO, XVIII, 1975, No. 2, p. 154.

[33] Cf. also PRU, III, 16.157, where a privileged person in royal service, a *mūdu Aziru*, is also: 22) *iš-tu qâti*M amel*akil* iṣ*narkabti ù* amel*ḫa-za-ni* 23) *za-ki* . . . ("22) from the hands of the overseer of the chariots and of the *ḫazannu* 23) he is free . . ."); in PRU, III, 16.250, a certain *Ilumilku*, also a royal *mūdu:* 18) *iš-tu qâti*ti amel*akil* iṣ*narkabti* 19) *ù* amel*ḫa-za-ni za-ki* ("19) from the hands of the overseer of the chariots 20) and from the *ḫazannu* he is free"); PRU, III, 16.348, gives details about the privileges of a *mūdu* of the queen, *Yanḫamu*, and also the: 10) amel*ḫa-a[z-z]a-nu a-na bîti-šu ul[irrub]* ("10) the *ḫazannu* shall not enter his house"). In all these cases the word *âlu*, "village," is completely lacking.

^{al}*Bêlet-re-mi li-pu-šu* 20) *ù a-na* ^{amel}*ḫa-za-ni* 21) *ša* ^{al}*Ša-al-mi-ya* 22) *a-na qâti*^{ti}*-šu šu-ku-un-šu-nu-ti* 23) *ù ma-am-ma lu-ú la-a* 24) *ú-ḫa-ab-ba-at-šu-nu-ti* 25) *a-di i-na ḫuršāni i-la-ku-ma* 26) *a-na pa-ni-šu-nu ma-am-ma* 27) *lu-ú la-a e-el-li* 28) *ú-nu-te lil-la-pi mi-nu-um-me-e* 29) *e-re-šu an-[a š]a-am-mi* 30) ^{amel}*ḫa-za-nu ša Šal-mi-ya* 31) *li-di-in-na-šú-nu-ti.*

"14) And now: 15) concerning (metal) casters, 16) sons (people) of (the village) *Paništau*, 17) I write to you. 18) They have to make their offerings 19) into (the village) *Beletremi.*[34] 20) And to the charge of the *ḫazannu* 21) of (the village) *Šalmiya* 22) you must deliver them. 23) And nobody shall 24) plunder them[35] 25) when they will enter the mountains. 26) In their presence nobody 27) shall 28) strive himself after[36] (something). 29) The demand of food[37] (for them) 30): *the ḫazannu* of *Šalmiya* 31) has to give it them."

Although some passages of the text are not definitively clear, we learn that people from the village *Paništau,* from the kingdom of Ugarit, had to make their sacrifices at *Beletremi,* outside the kingdom. On their way, the *ḫazannu* of the Ugaritic village *Šalmiya* had to protect them and give them assistance.

It is clear that every *ḫazannu* was a *ḫazannu âli,* "*ḫazannu* of the village." He was a royal official, but it is unclear to what degree he was connected with the local communal authorities or self-government. It is only clear that privileged royal servicemen were, at least sometimes, freed from his jurisdiction. The *ḫazannu* was an official. But, even the comparative data from the Hittite Empire and Canaan of the El-Amarna period does not give us a definitive answer about all the functions and prerogatives of the *ḫazannu.*[37a]

2. *Rb.* We do not know the exact Ugaritic counterpart of the Akkadian term *ḫazannu,* but *rb* is one of the possible alternatives. The literal meaning of the word is "big," "great." In the list found in PRU, II, 24 (UT, 1024) Rev. 3) "one great of the village" *(rb. qrt. aḥd)* is mentioned. PRU, V, 8, 3 (UT, 2008) is a letter written to the king in the name of the *rb* of a

---

[34] Unknown as a village of the kingdom of Ugarit. Perhaps it was outside the confines of the kingdom but inside the Hittite zone of political influence.

[35] AHW, pp. 303–4, contrary to the translation of *J. Nougayrol,* U. V, p. 93, footnote 4, "shall not impose a tax."

[36] "To strive (stretch) himself." Cf. AHW, p. 199, *elēpu(m),* "sprießen." Although the word concerns mainly the growing of plants, it is the only possible translation. *J. Nougayrol,* U, V, p. 94, note 1, "inconnu"; cf. also *Berger,* UF, II, 1970, p. 286 *līlepu* = "Teil des Pferdegeschirrs anzusetzen."

[37] *Berger,* UT, II, 1970, p. 286, No. 263, line 29.

[37a] *H. Otten,* Aufgaben eines Bürgermeisters in *Ḫattuša,* BM, 3, 1964, pp. 91–95.

village.[38] The text itself talks about naval affairs. The term *rb* was used for designating "elders" or "chiefs" of various groups of royal servicemen, e.g., *rb khnm* ("elder of the priests"), *rb nqdm* ("elder of the shepherds"), *rb ḥršm* ("elder of the construction workers"), *rab malaḫḫē*ᴹ ("elder of the seamen"), etc. Except for the naval affairs discussed in PRU, V, 8, we know nothing about the activities of the *rb* of the villages. It is unclear what sort of relations existed between the *rb* and the other branches of the local self-government.

3. *Skn*—(Akk. ᵃᵐᵉˡ*sākinu*). This is sometimes written as *MAŠKIM*.[39] Although this term sometimes means the "vizier" (of the whole kingdom) *(sākin mâti)*, we may consider only the *skn qrt—sākin âli*, the village official. According to text PRU, II, 33 (UT, 1033), which is a "list of *blblm*" *(spr blblm)*,[40] the *skn* of (the villages) *Uškn, Šbn, Ubrᶜ*, and *Ḫrṣbᶜ* received a certain number of clothes from the royal stores. A *skn* of *Ul[m]* is also known from the sources.[41]

The tablet PRU, V, 11 (UT, 2011) lists, among other people, *bnš mlk* ("royal dependents" (servicemen)) who received food rations *(ḥpr)* in the month of *Iṯt[bnm]* (line 1). Listed also are: 10) *ᶜpṯrm. Šmᶜrgm. skn. qrt* 11) *Ḥgbn. Šmᶜ. skn. qrt.* "10) *ᶜpṯrm* (people)[42]—*Šmᶜrgm—skn* of village 11) *Ḥgbn* (and) *Šmᶜ skn's* of villages."[43] To what villages they belonged is unknown. The text shows clearly that the *skn qrt* were "royal dependents."

---

[38] 3) *tḥm. rb Mi[ḫd (or-[dḫ]) ᶜ]bdh* ("the message of the great of *Mi[ḫd]* (or *Mi[dḫ]*), your servant"). The names of both villages are known in Ugarit. The reading of *C. H. Gordon*, UT, p. *4 *rb mi[t]* ("head of hundr[ed] (men)") has no precedence in the texts and is unconvincing.

[39] This sumerogramm is usually read as *râbiṣu*, but in Syria in the Amarna age, and in Ugarit, it is to be read as *sākinu*. Cf. Hebr. *sōken*, Phoen. *skn; W. F. Albright*, Two Little Unterstood Amarna Letters from the Middle of the Jordan Valley, BASOR, 89, 1943, pp. 7–17; *G. Buccellati*, Due noti ai testi Accadici di Ugarit, OA, II, 1963, No. 2, pp. 224–28; *MAŠKIM-sākinu, A. F. Rainey*, ᴸᵁ*MAŠKIM* at Ugarit, Or 35, 1961, pp. 426–28; *Heltzer*, Carskaya Administraciya, p. 222, —a preliminary study on the *skn/sākinu* of the *âlu/qrit; E. Lipinski, Skn* et *Sgn* dans le semitique occidental du Nord, UF, III, 1973, pp. 191–207.

[40] Meaning unclear. WUS, p. 49, No. 518; UT, p. 372, No. 420; *Dietrich, Loretz*, BiOr, 23, 1966, p. 129, suppose that it could be the designation of people delivering their grain-tax(?), but in our opinion, the text is talking about delivery from the royal stores of *ktt*, "clothes," for royal dependents.

[41] PRU, II, 93 (UT, 1093) 6) *skn Ul[m]* 9) *sk[n . . .]*. The poor state of preservation of this text precludes the possibility of further conclusions.

[42] The meaning of this designation of the professional group is unclear. (Cf. UT, p. 460, No. 1902.)

[43] Plur. st. cstr.

We also know that *Iribilu*, the *sākinu* of *Riqdi*,[44] dealt with the withdrawal of lands from the *nayyālu* in his village and had the right to hand the land over to another person. The *sākinu (MAŠKIM) Ukulliilanu*, of the village *Miḫi*,[45] appears as a witness in one document. *Entašalu*, the *sākinu (MAŠKIM)* of the *âlu Bêru*, received the rights to collect the taxes of the village in his own favour.[46] Thus, we have additional confirmation that the *sākinu* of certain villages were not elected by the self-government, but were royal dependents.[47] The very fact that, in *Ilštmᶜ*, royal fields distributed to servicemen were in the hands of the *skn* is an additional proof that the *sākinu* were royal officials.[48]

In conclusion, the analysis of the above terms, *ḫazannu*, *rb*, and *skn*, indicates that the difference of synonymy of these terms is as yet unclear. This is because these terms do not appear together in the same text. What is clear is that these officials were not elected members of the local population. They were dependents of the king. Thus, even the councils of the elders were far from democratic institutions being composed, most likely, of representatives of some of the more prominent families.

---

[44] U, V, 9 (RS. 17.61). For more about this text and its full translation cf. Ch. IV, pp. 55–56.

[45] PRU, IV, 17.28, 26.

[46] PRU, III, 16.244. Cf. Ch. III, p. 49 for more details about the tablet.

[47] Taking into account the fact that we have no data to indicate that *skn qrt* governed more than one village, and that at least eight *sākinu* of villages are named together with the village under their governance, we must drop the notion that these *sākinu* governed districts which were independent before merging with Ugarit (*J. Aistleitner*, Lexikalisches zu den ugaritischen Texten, AOH, XI, 1960, 1–3, p. 34).

[48] PRU, II, 104, 1–2) *šd. ubdy. Ilštmᶜ. dt. bd. skn* ("The service-fields in *Ilštmᶜ*, which are in the hands of the *skn*"); a list of the fields follows.

CHAPTER VII

PROPERTY RELATIONS WITHIN THE RURAL COMMUNITY

As shown above, the rural community of the kingdom of Ugarit was not based on equal division of property among its members. We also see that certain families became *nayyālu* and were deprived of their land. Several properties were divided among several persons (cf. below). Land transactions between private persons took place also, and, at least in several cases, we are dealing with relatively rich people who possessed much land, cattle, slaves, and other property. The council of elders of the village was in the hands of some of the prominent families.

For people who lost their land, the only way to survive was to enter the royal service and become royal dependents *(bnš mlk)*. People who bought land became members of the community in which the land was situated. But, as we have seen above, foreigners did not have the right to purchase land. Our task in this chapter is to try to discover how property relations developed within the community among certain families, provided that they were not *nayyālu*, and did not sell or lose their property.

The Evolution of Property Relations

We have three tablets on which to base our analysis: PRU, V, 44 (UT, 2044), PRU, II, 80 (UT, 1080), and CTC, 81 (UT, 329). All three texts mention the same families, but their property ownership changes from one text to another. The references to the same persons in all three texts proves that although these texts were composed at different times, the recorded data spans the lifetime of one generation.[1] Unfortunately, it is impossible to establish the correct chronological order of these texts. We will use PRU, V, 44 as the basic text because it is in the best state of preservation.[2]

PRU, V, 44	PRU, II, 80	CTC, 81
1) *yd(?). [ ]*	—	—
2) *a[ ]m[ ]n. a[ ]*	—	—
3) *w. a[ṯṯ]h. [ ]*[3]	—	—

[1] Cf. also, the fragment PRU, V, 142, which lists families. A partial analysis of these texts is made by *M. Heltzer*, VDI, 1966, No. 3, pp. 203–204.

[2] Unless otherwise specified the reading is according to *C. H. Gordon* in UT.

4) Ḫzmtn. ṯn[bnh waṯth][3]	—	—
5) w. ṯlṯ. alph. [	—	—
6) Swn. qrty. w. [b]nh[ ]	12) Swn. qrty. w[. aṯth]	8) Swn. qrty[aṯth wbnh][3]
7) w. alph. w. a[r]bᶜ. l. arbᶜ[m ṣin][3]	13) [w]. bnh. w. ṯn alpm	9) uḫh. w. ᶜšr[ṣinh][3]
	14) [w] ṯlṯm. ṣin	
8) Pln. ṯmry. w. ṯn. bnh. w[	9) Pln. [ṯmry]	
	10) w. ṯn. bn[h w. . . .]	
9) Ymrn. apsny [.] w. aṯth . . . bn[h]		
10) Prd. mᶜqby [. w.] a]ṯth[ ]	11) [Pr]d mᶜqby[waṯth][3]	
11) Prt. mgd[ly. w. ṯt(?).] at[th		
12) ᶜdyn[waṯth[3]]		
13) w. ṯn[bnh]		
14) Iwrm[w][3] bn[h[3]]		
rev.) Annt[n] w[aṯth[3]]		
16) w. ṯn. bnh. [ ]		
17) Aǵltn. ypr[y waṯth wbnh]-	7) Aǵltn. [ypr]y. w. [aṯth]	
18) w. šbᶜ. ṣinh[ ]	8) w. bnh w. alp. w. [ṣinh(?)]	
	1) [A]ḏmu . apsty . b[ ]	
	2) w . bnh . w. aṯth . w. alp w . ṯmn . ṣin	
	3) [Y][3]dln. qmnzy. w. a[ṯth]	
	4) w . ṯn . bnh	
	5) Ṯmgdl. yknᶜmy . w. aṯth	
	6) w . bnh . w . alp . aḥd	
	15) Annḏr . yknᶜmy	
	16) w . aṯth . w. bnh	
	17) w . alp . w. tš[ᶜ] ṣin	
		1) Ḥ[3]dd. ar[y]
		2) Bᶜlsip a[ry wbnh]
		3) klth. [ ]

[3] Our reconstruction, based on analogy in the parallel texts.

		4) *Ṯty. ary. m[ ]*
		5) *Nrn arny [ ]*
		6) *w. ṯn. bnh. w. [ ]*
		7) *b tn [ ]*
		10) *Klyn. apsn[y]*
		11) *Plzn.qrty[wbnh*[3]*]*
		12) *w. klth. b. t[ ]*
PRU, V, 44	PRU, II, 80	CTC. 81
		rev.) *Bᶜly. mlk[wbnh(?)]*
		14) *yd. bth. yd[ ]*
		15) *Ary. yd. t[bth]*[4]
		16) *ḫtnh. Šbᶜl [ ]*
		17) *Ṯlḥny. yd [x bnh]*
		18) *yd. ṯlṯ. kl[th*[5] *]*
		19) *w. ṯṯm. ṣi[n]*
		20) *t n[ ]*
		21) *Agyn. [ ]*
		22) *[ ]. tn. [ ]*

PRU, V, 44

(Lines 1–3 illegible)

4) *Ḫẓmtn*, two [his sons and his wife] 5) and his three oxen [ ]

6) *Swn*, man of (the village) *Qrt* and his [s]on [and his wife]
7) and his ox and [fou]rty fo[ur small cattle][6]

8) *Pln* man of (the village) *Ṯmr* and his two sons, and[7] [. . .]

9) *Ymrn*, man of (the village) *Apsn* and his wife . . . [and his] son[. . .]

10) *Prd*, man of (the village) *Mᶜqb* [and] his wif[e . . .][8]

11) *Prt*, [man] of (the village) *Mgdl* [and two(?)[9] his] wives

12) *ᶜdyn* [and his wife . . .] 13) and [his] two [sons . . .]

[4] "His daughter" *(bth)* must precede the word *ḫtn*, "son-in-law."

[5] *klt*—Hebr. *kallā*—cf. line 12 of the same text. Three "daughters-in-law" indicates from one to three husbands, sons of the *Ṯlḥny*. The reading *ṯlṯ kl[bm]*, "three dogs," is unacceptable.

[6] PRU, II, 80, "12) *Swn* man of (the village) *Qrt* and [his wife] 13) [and] his son and two oxen 14) [and] thirty small cattle." CTC, 81, "8) *Swn*, man of (the village) *Qrt* [his wife and his son], 9) his brother and ten [small cattle ?]."

[7] PRU, II, 80, "9) [man of (the village) *Ṯmr*] and [his] two sons [and . . .]."

[8] PRU, II, 80, "11) *[Pr]d*, man of (the village) *Mᶜqb* [and his wife]."

[9] The reconstruction of *C. H. Gordon*, without explanation.

14) *Iwrm* [and his] son [ ]

15) *Annt[n]* and [his wife . . .] 16) and his two sons [ ]

17) *Ağltn* [man] of (the village) *Yp*[*r* and his wife and his son] 18) and his seven small cattle [ ][10]

PRU, II, 80 (without paralleling passages)

1) *[A]d̠mu*, man of (the village) *Apsn* in [ ] 2) and his son, and his wife, and an ox, and eight small cattle.

3) *[Y]dln*, man of (the village) *Qmnz*, and [his wi]fe, 4) and his two sons.

5) *Ṯmgdl*, man of (the village) *Yknᶜm*, and his wife, 6) and his son, and one ox.

15) *Annd̠r*, man of (the village) *Yknᶜm* 16) and his wife, and his son
17) and an ox, and nin[e] small cattle.

CTC, 81 (without parallel passages)

1) *Ḥdd.* [man] of (the village) *Ar* [and . . .]

2) *Bᶜlsip* [man of] (the village) *A*[*r* . . . and his son] 3) (and) his daughter-in-law [. . .]

4) *Ṯty*, man of (the village) *Ar* [ ]

5) *Nrn*, man of (the village) *Arn* [. . .] 6) and his two sons and [. . .]
7) . . . [ ]

10) *Klyn*, man of (the village) *Apsn* [and . . .]

11) *Plzn*, man of (the village) *Qrt* [. . . and his son] 12) and his daughter-in-law in *T[ ]*

13) *Bᶜly* [man] (of the village) *Mlk* [. . . and his wife] 14) together with his daughter, together [ ]

15) Man of (the village) *Ar* together with . . . [. . . his daughter]
16) son-in-law. *Šbᶜl* [ ]

17) The man of (the village) *Ṯlḥn*, together with [. . .] (and) x his sons
18) together with three [his] daughter-in-[law . . .] 19) and sixty small cat[tle . . .]
20) . . . [ ]

21) *Agyn.* [ ] 22) [ ] two [ ]

Listed here are at least twenty-five heads of families. Unfortunately, the text is broken and we cannot draw conclusions about the sizes of the families, and number of cattle possessed by these families. It is also clear that these texts contained nothing about land-property . . . Perhaps the

[10] PRU, II, 80, "7) *Ağltn*, man of (the village) *Ypr* and [his wife], 8) and his son and ox and [small cattle ?]."

amount of land possessed by these families remained constant, and therefore was not recorded in the lists. On the other hand, the number of cattle, as well as the size of the family, underwent certain changes. Therefore, such lists were rewritten, as we see from the documents presented here. Possibly, they were composed for tax-purposes, or to define the amount of corvée-service they had to perform.

The twenty-five (twenty-four) families are designated as people of at least twelve different villages: *Ar(y), Arn, Qrt, Ṯmr, Apsn(t), Mᶜqb, Mgdl, Ypr, Mlk, Ṯlḥn, Qmnz, Yknᶜm.*[11]

It is characteristic that, beside the head of the household, there is mentioned only his wife and his son(s), sometimes his daughter and son-in-law, as well as his daughter-in-law. We have to conclude that children who could not be considered as serious labourers were not mentioned in the text, which listed only adults. The mention of a son-in-law shows that, in certain cases, he entered the house of the father-in-law. Perhaps this was connected with the fact that the head of the family did not have sons. Completely lacking is any mention about slaves in the possession of these families. Perhaps these families did not possess them.

On the other hand, we see that the number of adult sons, who did not yet begin independent households, was small, from 1–3, and the same can be said of daughters. Only once is a brother of the head of the family mentioned. Generally speaking, we are not dealing with large patronymies, but with small individual families, although married children were not necessarily excluded.

Cattle is not designated in every family, perhaps partly because of the poor state of the text making recognition impossible. But we see that the number of oxen in one household varied from 1–3, and small cattle from 6–60.

Concerning the evolution of property, we can state that *Swn*, man of *Qrt*, had in one case one ox and forty-four small cattle, and in the second case two oxen and thirty small cattle. In the third case he had only ten small cattle. *Aǵltn*, man of *Ypr* had in one case seven small cattle, and in the second case one ox and x small cattle.

Such a difference in the number of cattle in the possession of various persons, as well as in the possession of the same persons, at different times, is also confirmed by the text PRU, V, 39 (UT, 2039) (cf. Ch. II, pp. 43–44) where five people of the village *Ṯlṯ* paid from five to ten small cattle each as their tax.

---

[11] After 5 personal names the place-name of their origin is broken.

Additional Lists of Families of the Villagers

We must exclude from this study the texts listing the families of royal dependents. The number of lists mentioning the villagers of Ugarit with their families is limited.

PRU, V, 80 (UT, 2080)

1) *bn. Bʿln. Biry* 2) *ṯlṯ bʿlm* 3) *w. adnkm. ṯr. w. arbʿ. bnth.*

4) *Yrḫm. yd. ṯn. bnh* 5) *bʿlm. w. ṯlṯ. nʿrm. w. bt. aḥt.*

6) *bn. Lwn. ṯlṯtm. bʿlm*

7) *bn. Bʿly. ṯlṯtm. bʿlm* 8) *w. aḥd. ḫbṯ* 9) *w. arbʿ. aṯt*

10) *bn. Lg. ṯn. bnh* 11) *bʿlm. w. aḫth* 12) *b Šrt.*

13) *Šty. w. bnh.*

"1) *Bn. Bʿln,* man of (the village) *Bir,* 2) three workmen,[12] 3) and their lord (may be overseer) *Ṯr,*[12a] and his four daughters

4) *Yrḫm,* together with his two sons, 5) two workmen,[13] and three youths[14] and one doughter.

6) *Bn. Lwn,* six[15] workmen.

7) *Bn. Bʿly,* six[15] workmen, 8) and one *ḫupšu*-man[16] 9) and four wives (or "women").

10) *Bn. Lg.* two sons, 11) two workmen, and his sister, in (the village) *Šrt.*

11) *Šty* and his son."

This text consists of a list of six families. One family was from the village of *Bir*, another was from *Šrt*. The wife (or wives) of the head of the family are not always mentioned. But other members of the family, sons, daughters, and various categories of dependents, are listed. They are *nʿrm* "youth," *bʿlm* "workmen," *ḫupšu*. No maidens are mentioned, including daughters who were not yet married. The number of sons per family was 1–2, daughters, up to four. In one case, the head of the family

[12] Cf. *Ch. Virolleaud*, PRU, V, p. 106, on the interchange of *b*/*p* in Ugaritic; *bʿl*/*pʿl*, *P. Fronzaroli*, La fonetica Ugaritica, Rome, 1953; *C. H. Gordon*, UT, pp. 35–5.28; p. 375, No. 494; *Leslau*, Observations, p. 351; *M. Weippert*, UF, VI, 1974, p. 417.

[12a] *ṯr*—here a personal name—cf. ZUL, XI, p. 38, No. 117.

[13] Dual form.

[14] May be children, but "dependents" also possible. Cf. Biblical-Hebrew *naʿar; M. Heltzer*, Slaves, p. 86.

[15] *ṯlṯtm*, "three" in the dual form.

[16] *ḫb*/*pt*—Akk. [amel]*ḫupšu*—the exact sense of this term in Ugarit is not clear; a kind of dependent people; a analysis of this term is found in ZUL, XI, pp. 26–27, No. 44.

has an unmarried sister in his house. It also seems that minor children were not mentioned. It is also important that the text comes from the royal archives. This underlines the fact that these people had to pay taxes and perform their corvée. Neither the land nor the cattle of these people is mentioned here.

It is significant that the twenty-five families listed in the three texts given above, had no slaves or dependents. At the same time, of the six families mentioned in PRU, V, 80 (UT. 2080), five of them had such dependents. Five families out of the total of thirty-one represents 17 percent of the families which had dependents. The total number of dependents was twenty-three, thus, there were 4,5 persons per family-household. Unfortunately, it is impossible to say whether such an average gives us a true picture of the size and structure of the household in the villages of the kingdom of Ugarit.

We have also seen above (Ch. IV, pp. 52–58) that such people lost their land to the royal authorities if they became debtors or did not perform their obligations. They could also be taken abroad as slaves in cases where they could not repay their debts to foreign creditors. But even in such cases, their lands, as seen from text PRU, IV, 17.130, remained in the hands of the king of Ugarit; it was not turned over to foreigners. The fact that royal servicemen received land-holdings in Ugarit is not in contradiction with this.[17] Such royal servicemen could become Ugaritians through land purchase, but only if they were royal dependents *(bnš mlk)* of the king of Ugarit.

The Relation of Individual Households to the Community

As we have seen above, in the *nayyālu*-texts (Ch. IV, pp. 52–56), people who, in some cases, received land-holdings which were community lands withdrawn from the *nayyālu*, had to perform the "corvée of his house" *(pil-ku bîti-šu, or unušša-bîti)*.[18]

Naturally, such family possessions could be sold,[19] bought, and in-

[17] Cf. *A. F. Rainey*, A Social Structure, pp. 87–91. Rainey makes no difference between holdings and property and, therefore, he states that foreigners were landowners in the kingdom of Ugarit.

[18] PRU, III, 15.89, 20–21; 16.262, 10–11.

[19] *R. Haase*, Anmerkungen zum ugaritischen Immobilienkauf, ZA, 14 (58), 1967, pp. 196–210—all documents including PRU, IV; *M. Heltzer*, Some Questions of the Agrarian Relations in Ugarit, VDI, 1960, No. 2, 86–90 (Russian); additional tablets U, V, 4 (RS. 17.20); 6 (RS. 17.149); 159 (RS. 17.86); 160 (RS. 17.102); 161 (RS.

herited[20] within the community. Unfortunately, we do not always know, when such transactions were made, in which *âlu/qrt* they occured. But the formulae referring to the obligations of the house clearly point out that it was within a certain village—a rural community.

1. PRU, III, 15.156 relates that a woman *Batrabi*, and *Šubammu*, both "children of (a women) Layawa" *(m[ârē]^{M} ^{f}La-ya-a-wa)* sold 20 *iku* of land in ^{al}*Ṭibaqu* to a "(women) *Talaya*, daughter of [x] *(^{f}Ta-la-ya mârat [x])* for 420 sheqels of silver. Further, it is said that 11) *i[l-ka ù] píl[-ka ^{I}Šu-ub-am-mu ù]* 12) *[^{f}Bat-ra]-ab-i [ubbalu(?)]* 13) *[^{I}Š]u-ub-am-mu* 14) *[ù] ^{I}Bat-ra-ab-i* 15) *u-nu-uš-ša u-ba-lu.*

"11) the *il*[*ku*-service (corvée) and] *píl*]-*ku* service (corvée) *Šubammu* and] 12) *[Batr]abi* [shall perform]. 13) *[Š]ubammu* 14) [and] *Batrabi* 15) shall perform the *unuššu*-service (corvée)."[21]

Most interesting in this text is that the obligations remain on the responsibility of the former owners of the land. They have to perform the obligations, and they formally remain the community members. The question is, who received the rights?

2. PRU, III, 16.14. According to this text, *Nuriyanu* (the brother of the king) made an exchange of land with a certain *Laya*. *Laya* gave *Nuriyanu*, not his own field, but one of his holdings, the field of *Abdinikal*, son of *Ananiya*. As a result of the exchange, "11) *Nuriyanu* was free 12) from the *pilku* of the house of *Abdinikal*." (11) *ù-za-ki ^{I}Nu-ri-ya-nu* 12) *iš-tu píl-ki bît ^{I}Abdi-ni-kal.*) This may indicate that one of the former owners *(Laya* or *Abdinikal)* had to perform this service.[22]

3. PRU, III, 16.167. This text relates that king *Niqmaddu* II handed over the lands of two persons to *Anatešub*. The latter had to pay to the king 200 sheqels of silver, as also "he performs the *unuššu* of the houses (households)." (17) *ù u-nu-ša bîta-ti^{M} ub-bal.*) So *Anatešub* took upon himself the former owners' obligations within the community. We do not know in which *âlu* these households were located.

4. PRU, III, 15.123. We learn from this text that two persons, *Anatenu* and *Yayanu*, son of *Ayalu*, made a land exchange. *Anatenu*

17.325)—the latter are three cases are land purchases by the queen-mother of Ugarit; PRU, VI, 40 (RS. 17.360).

[20] *Fr. Thurean-Dangin*, Trois contrats de Ras Shamra, "Syria," XVIII, 1937, p. 249, RS. 8. 145, The Testament of *Yarimanu*.

[21] *ilku/pilku/unuššu*, cf. Ch. IV note 4; the difference between these terms is not yet recognized. The latest study is by *M. Dietrich, O. Loretz, Pilku = Ilku* "Lehnspflicht," UF, IV, 1972, pp. 165–66, but it does not explain the etymology of the term.

[22] Cf. PRU, III, 16.133, a fragment where, according to the remnants of the text, the problem could be the same.

added [x] sheqels of silver for the more valuable field he received from *Yayanu*. But *Yayanu* remained obligated in that "he had to perform the *pilku*-service of his house(hold)." (18) *ù* ^{I}*Ya-ya-nu píl-ka* 19) *bîti-ša ub-bal.)*

5. PRU, III, 16.246. A land-exchange between *Ḫuttenu*, son of *Aḫa-maranu*, and *Yapašarru*, son of *Sinaru*, is the subject of this text. The text states that, "his *pilku*-service of these fields *Yapašarru* shall not perform." (15) *ù pilka-šu ša eqlāti*^{M} *šu-wa-ti* 11) ^{I}*Yapa-šarru ú-ul ú-bal.)*[23]

6. We also know of purely private land transactions inside the community. PRU, III, 15.136 mentions a certain *Kalbiya*, son of *Kabityanu*, who sold six *iku* for 520 sheqels to a certain *Kurwanu*, son of *Baalazki*. The lands were totally freed from *pilku*-service.[24]

7. PRU, III, 16.154. This text demands more serious consideration.

1) *iš-tu ûmi*^{mi} *an-ni-im* 2) *a-na pa-ni* ^{I}*Am-mis-tam-ru mâr Niq-me-pa* 3) *šàr* ^{al}*Ú-ga-ri-it*^{KI} 4) ^{I}*Abdi-milku mâr Din-ni-ya* 5) *ip-šu-ur eqil*^{M}*-šu* $^{\mathrm{i\check{s}}}$*karāni*^{M}*-šu* 6) $^{\mathrm{i\check{s}}}$*serdi*^{M}*-šu* $^{\mathrm{b\hat{i}t}}$*dimta-šu* 7) *ša i-na* ^{nar}*Na-aḫ-ra-ya* 8) *a-na* ^{f}*Um-mi-ḫi-bi* 9) *i-na 7 me-at 40 kaspi*^{M} 10) *eqlu*^{M} *ṣa-mi-id i-na* ^{il}*Šamši ûmi*^{mi} 11) *a-na* ^{f}*Um-mi-ḫi-bi* 12) *ù a-na mârē*^{M}*-ša* 13) *a-di da-ri-ti* 14) *amêlu ma-am-ma-an ul i-la-qi-šu* 15) *iš-tu qâti*^{ti} ^{f}*Um-mi-ḫi-bi* 16) *ù iš-tu qâti*^{ti} *mârē*^{M}*-ša* 17) *ù píl-ka ya-nu i-na eqli*^{M} *an-ni-i ša* ^{nar}*Na-aḫ-ra* 18) *ša-ni-tam* ^{I}*Píl-su ù* ^{I}*Abdi-milku* 19) *2 mâr* ^{I}*Aḫi-milku* 20) *ip-šu-ru-nim 2 ikî ½ eqla*^{H} 21) *qa-du* $^{\mathrm{i\check{s}}}$*serdi*^{M}*-šu* 22) *i-na eqli*^{M} ^{nar}*Na-aḫ-ra-ya* 23) *a-na* $^{\mathrm{[f]}}$*Um-mi-ḫi-bi* 24) *i-na 1 me-at 30 kaspi*^{M} 25) *2 ikû ½ eqlu*^{M} *an-nu-ú ṣa-mi-id i-na* ^{il}*Šamši ûmi*^{mi} 26) *a-na* ^{f}*Um-mi-ḫi-bi ù a-na mârē*^{M}*-ša a-di da-ri-ti* 27) *amêlu ma-am-ma-an la i-la-qi-šu* 28) *iš-tu qâti*^{ti} ^{f}*Um-mi-ḫi-bi* 29) *ù iš-tu qâti*^{ti} *mârē*^{M}*-ša* 30) *ù píl-ka ya-nu i-na 2 ikî ½ eqli*^{M} *an-ni-i* 31) ^{aban}*kunuk* ^{I}*A-mis-tam-ri mâr Niq-me-pa* 32) *šàr* ^{al}*Ú-ga-ri-it.*

"1) From the present day, 2) before *Ammistamru*, son of *Niqmepa*, 3) King of Ugarit: 4) *Abdimilku*, son of *Dinniya* 5) sold his field, his vineyard, 6) his olivetrees, his *dimtu* (farmhouse), 7) which are located (in the district) of the river *Naḫraya*, 8) to *Ummiḫibi* 9) for 740 (sheqels) of silver. 10) The field is in the possession— as the daylight— 11) of *Ummiḫibi* 12) and her sons 13) forever. 14) Nobody shall take (it away) 15) from *Ummiḫibi* 16) and from her sons. 17) And these fields in the district of *Naḫra* have no *pilku* (service). 18) Further: *Pilsu* and *Abdimilku*, 19) two sons of *Aḫimilku* 20) sold 2.5 *iku* of field 21) together with their olive trees 22) located (in the district) of *Naḫraya* 23) to *Ummiḫibi* 24) for 130

[23] Cf. also, the damaged tablet PRU, III, 15.143.

[24] Cf. also, PRU, III, 15.145—a land transaction with total exemption from *pilku*-service. See also PRU, III, 15.140; 16.134; 16.256.

(sheqels) of silver. 25) These 2.5 *iku* of field are 26) —like daylight— in the possession of *Ummiḫibi* and her sons forever. 27) Nobody shall take it 28) from *Ummiḫibi* 29) and from her sons. 3) And these 2.5 *iku* of field have no *pilku*-service. 31) The seal of *Ammistamru*, son of *Niqmepa*, 32) king of Ugarit."

In this text we have seen that *Ummiḫibi* purchased two plots of land in the same district. But, the land was free from labour or service. Whether the land was totally free, or the former owners sold only a part of their land and continued to perform their obligations as previously, is not definitively clear. It seems that the latter possibility is more reasonable. It is partially confirmed by the text PRU, III, 16.343.

1) *iš-tu ûmi*^{mi} *an-ni-im* 2) *a-na pa-ni* ^{I}*A-mis-tam-ri mâr Niq-me-pa* 3) *šàr* ^{al}*Ú-ga-ri-it*^{KI} 4) ^{f}*Um-mi-ḫi-bi ti-it-ta-aš-ši* 5) *eqla qa-du* ^{bit}*dimti-šu* ^{iṣ}*karāni*^{M}*-šu* ^{iṣ}*serdi*^{M}*-šu* 6) *ša i-na Iš-ši-qi* 7) *ù ti-it-ta-din-šu-na* 8) *a-na* ^{I}*A-na-te-na mâr Aš-mu-wa-na* 9): *ta-ap-de*$_4$*-ti eqli*^{M}*-šu* 10) *ù* ^{I}*A-na-te-nu mâr Aš-mu-wa-na* 11) *it-ta-aš-ši eqla*^{M}*-šu* ^{iṣ}*karani*^{M}*-šu* 12) *qa-du* ^{bit}*dimti-šu* ^{iṣ}*serdi*^{M}*-šu* 13) *ša i-na Na-[a]ḫ-ra-ya* 14) *ù it-ta-din-š[u-n]u* 15) *a-na* ^{f}*Um-mi-ḫi-bi* 16) *eqlu*^{H} *ṣa-mi-id a-na* ^{f}*Um-mi-ḫi-bi* 17) *ù a-na mârē*^{M}*-ša ù píl-ka-šu ya-nu* 18) *ù* ^{I}*A-na-te-nu pil-ka bîti-šu* 19) *ù-ba-al* 20) ^{aban}*kunuk* ^{I}*A-mis-tam-ri mâr Niq-me-pa* 21) *šàr* ^{al}*Ú-ga-ri-it.*

"1) From the present day: 2) before *Ammistamru*, son of *Niqmepa*, 3) King of Ugarit: 4) *Ummiḫibi* withdrew 5) the field, together with her *dimtu* (farmhouse), her vineyard, her olive trees,[25] 6) which are located in (the village) *Iššiqi*[26] 7) and gave them 8) to *Anatena*, son of *Ašmuwana* 9) —as an exchange of his field. 10) And *Anatenu*, son of *Ašmuwanu* 11) withdrew his field, his vineyard, 12) together with his *dimtu*, his olive trees, 13) which are located in (the district) of *Naḫraya* 14) and gave them 15) to *Ummiḫibi*. 16) The field is in possession of *Ummiḫibi* 17) and of her sons. And there is no *pilku* (service-corvée) of it.[27] 18) And *Anatenu* has to perform the *pilku* 19) of his house. 20) Seal of *Ammistamru*, son of *Niqmepa*, 21) King of Ugarit."

Again, it is clear that *Ummiḫibi* received land free from corvée-service. At the same time, *Anatenu* had to perform the *pilku* (service or corvée) of his house. It also seems clear, that *Ummiḫibi* had the privilege of purchasing land, and, at the same time, was freed from obligations and taxes,

[25] The suffix, *-šu*, suff. pers. pron. 3 sg. masc. by mistake instead of *-ša*, suff. pers. pron. 3 sg. fem.

[26] *Iššiqi* or *Išqi*, a known Ugaritic village, appears here without the determinative.

[27] Of these fields.

while commoners, members of the rural community, had to perform or to deliver the service for their house, in the framework of the community obligations.

9. PRU, III, 16.261, dated by the same reign as the former text, relates that, 4) ^{f}*La-e-ya-a ù* $^{\mathrm{[I]il}}{}_{2}$*Addu-mi-iš-la-am* 5) *ù* ^{f}*Bat-ṣi-id-qi mâru*^{M}*-ša* 6) *íl-te-qu-ú eqla*^{M} 7) *ša* ^{I}*Ya-ap-lu-na* 8) *ù ša* ^{I}*Ḫi-iš-mi-ya-na* 9) *ù ša* ^{I}*Uz-zi-na* 10) *ú ša* ^{I}*Šu-ub-am-m[i]* 11) *mârē*^{M} ^{I}*S[à]-s[i]-y[a]-n[a* 12) *qa-du* ^{bit}*dimti*^{KI} *[. . .]* 13) *qa-du* ^{is}*serdi*$^{\mathrm{[M]}}$ 14) *qa-du* ^{is}*karāni*^{M} *[. . .]* 15) *qa-du gáb-bi [m]i-i[m-mu-šu]* 16) *i-na 2 li-im 2 me-at [. . . kaspi].*

"4) *Laeya* and *Addumišlam*, 5) and (the woman) *Batṣidqi*, her children 6) purchased the field 7) of *Yaplunu* 8) and of *Ḫišmiyanu* 9) and of *Uzzinu* 10) and of *Šubammu*— 11) the sons of *S[a]s[i]y[a]nu* 12) together with the *dimtu* (farmhouse), 13) together with the olive trees [. . .] 14) together with the vineyards [ ] 15) together with all they possess 16) for 2200 [(sheqels) of silver]."

According to the standard formulae of ownership, the text points out, 15) *ù píl-ku [y]a-a-nu* 26) *i-na eqli*^{M} *an-ni-i* ("and these fields have no *pilku* (service or corvée). The seal and name of the scribe are following.") Perhaps formerly, the owners had to perform certain obligations for these fields.

As we have seen, the households in the rural communities of Ugarit had to perform certain obligations. Naturally, they were those same obligations as were listed when we dealt with the community obligations as a whole.

The texts given above offer us a certain amount of information about landowning by small collectives of relatives. This brings us once more to the problem of patronymies in the rural communities of the kingdom of Ugarit. In order to better understanding of this problem we must analyze some additional texts.

10. PRU, III, 15.182. This tablet, badly damaged, relates, that at least two persons, who are designated as *mârē*^{M} *of [x]* ("sons of [x]"), sold to *Uzzina*, the *sākin mâti* ("the vizier of the land (of Ugarit)"), fields for ninety-five sheqels of silver. It is clear that the sellers were brothers.

11. U, V, 159 (RS. 17.86).

1) *iš-tu* ${}_{2}$*ûmi an-ni-i-im* 2) *a-na pa-ni* $^{\mathrm{amelM}}{}_{2}$*šîbūti*^{ti} 3) $^{\mathrm{I}}{}_{2}$*Ili*^{li}*-ya mâr* ^{I}*Si-ni-ya* 4) *ù* ^{I}*Pa-di-ya aḫa-šu* 5) *ù mârē*^{M}*-šu-nu* 6) *ip-šur-nim 4 eqil*^{M}*-šu-nu* 7) *ša i-na eqli*^{M} *Ṣa-i* 8) *i-na 1 me-at 80 kaspi*^{M} 9) *a-na* ^{f}*Šar-el-li* 10) *šarrati 4 eqlu*^{M} *ṣa-mi-id i-na* ^{il}*Šamši*^{šu} 12) ${}_{2}$*ûmi a-na* ^{f}*Šar-el-li šarrati* 13) *a-di da-ri-ti* (Lines 14–19 names the witness and the scribes).

"1) From the present day, 2) before the witnesses, 3) *Iliya*, son of *Siniya* 4) and *Padiya*, his brother 5) and their sons 6) sold 4 *(iku)* of their field 7) which are located among the fields of (the village) *Ṣaᶜu*.[28] 8) for 180 (sheqels) of silver 9) to *Šarelli*, 10) the queen.[29] 4 *(iku)* of field 11) are in the possession— like daylight— 12) of *Šarelli*, the queen 13) forever."

The text, U, V, 160 (RS. 17.102) is incorrectly written. The queen bought land from 3) *mâru*ru I*Pu-lu-lu-na* ("the son of *Pululuna*"), but the next line relates that, "he sold their fields" (4) *ip-šur eqil*M*-šu-nu*). Thus, it is possible that here we have a case, similar to those above, in which land was sold by a collective of owners-relatives.

The scarcity of the sources obscures the real number of larger families, patronymies, in the villages of the kingdom. When we take the lists of families given above (pp. 85–90) we see only that the number of brothers belonging to the family was not a large one. It is also impossible to deduce the real percentage of these patronymies. But, we see from the landsale transactions: a) (PRU, III, 15.156) a brother and sister sold their land, belonging to them collectively; b) (PRU, III, 16.154, 18ff.) two brothers sold their common land to the woman *Ummiḫibi;* c) (PRU, III, 16.261) One woman, together with her sons and daughter, purchased the land of four brothers, sons of *Sasiyanu;* d) (PRU, III, 15.182) Two brothers sold their collective land to *Uzzinu;* 3) (U, V, 159) Two brothers, together with their sons, sold their land to the queen (cf. U, V, 160 also).

Thus, we can see that, at least in some cases, there were traces of collective landownership by patronymies—the so-called "undivided brothers." It is also interesting to note, that women were among the purchasers of the land, as well as among the former owners. This feature is also known from other Ugaritic texts. It may be added, that in Ugarit the rights of women were almost the broadest in the ancient Near East.[30]

The presence of "undivided brothers," or to be more exact, "undivided families," among the basic population of the villages of Ugarit, also ap-

[28] The determinative is lacking.

[29] Ugar. *Ṯryl*, cf. *Nougayrol*, U, V, pp. 261–62; *Liverani*, Storia, p. 237ff. *Šarelli-Ṯryl* seems to be the queen-mother during the reign of *Ammistamru* II. On the role of the queen-mother in Ugarit, cf. *H. Donner*, Art und Herkunft des Amtes der Königin-Mutter im Alten Testament, Festschrift J. Friedrich zum 65. Geburtstag am 27. VIII. 1958, Heidelberg, 1959, pp. 105–45.

[30] *J. Klima*, Untersuchungen zum ugaritischen Erbrecht, ArOr, XXIV, 1956, pp. 356–74; *J. Klima*, Die Stellung der ugaritischen Frau, ArOr, XXV, 1957, pp. 313–33; *J. Klima*, Le statut de la femme a Ugarit d'apres les textes accadiens de Ras-Shamra, RSJB, XI, 1959, pp. 95–105.

pears in the documents concerning the division of property between children or brothers, or the disinheritance of some family members.

Division of Property and Disinheritance

In connection with this subject, we may take into account only those texts where we can establish that the owners were people of a village, or at least that they were not royal dependents *(bnš mlk)*.

1. PRU, III, 16.129.

1) *iš-tu ûmi*^{mi} *an-ni-i-im* 2) ^{I}*Ya-an-ḫa-nu mâr Ták-ka*$_{4}$*-na* 3) *ú-za-ki* ^{I}*Nu-ri-ya-na mâr-šu* 4) *iš-tu bîti*^{ti}*-šu iš-tu* 5) *eqlāti*^{M}*-šu iš-tu gab-bi mim-mu* 6) *ša* ^{I}*a-bi-šu*[31] *za-ka*$_{4}$ ^{I}*Nu-ri-ya-nu* 7) *ù 25 kaspu eli ša (?)* 8) ^{I}*Nu-ri-ya-na ša* 9) *[ši(?)]-ir-ku kasap (?)* ^{I}*a-bi-šu*[31] 10) *[šum-m]a ur-ra-am še-ra* 11) ^{amelM}*aḫḫe*^{M} *ša* ^{I}*Nu-ri-ya-na* 12) *i-tu-ur a-na* ^{I}*Nu-ri-ya* 13) *50 kaspu eli-šu-nu* 14) *ù šum-ma* ^{I}*Nu-ri-ya-nu* 15) *i-tu-ur a-na bît* ^{I}*a-bi-šu*[31] 16) *10 kaspu eli-šu* (Lines 17–19 state the names of the witnesses and the scribe.).

"1) From the present day, 2) *Yanḫanu*, son of *Takkana* 3) freed (lit. "purified") *Nuriyanu*, his son, 4) from his house, from 5) his fields, from all that 6) (belongs) to his father *Nuriyanu* is freed. 7) And 25 (sheqels) of silver to 8) *Nuriyanu* as 9) [the gi]ft of the silver of his father. 10) [I]f in future (lit. "tomorrow (and) after tomorrow") 11) the brothers of *Nuriyanu* 12) shall return to *Nuriya(nu)*—13) 50 (sheqels) of silver (he has to pay) to them. 14) And if *Nuriyanu* 15) returns to the house of his father 16) 10 (sheqels) of silver to him (he has to give, i.e. *Nuriyanu* has to pay his father)."

The text explains that *Nuriyanu* was deprived of his part of the property of his father's house, and received 50 sheqels of silver as compensation.

The property of the father was to be inherited by "his brothers." Thus, it is clear that no less than two sons remained in the father's house and both sides had the right to return to their former status. It is also clear, that the brothers of *Nuriyanu* did not intend to divide their property. The motives and reasons for this legal act are not comprehendable.

2. PRU, III, 15.90. This text was composed in the presence of king *Niqmaddu* II.

5) ^{I}*I-ḫi-ya-nu mâr Si-na-ra-na* 6) *zittē*^{M} *zi-te* 7) *ša* ^{amelM}*aḫḫe*^{M}*-šu* 8) *it-ta-din-ma-mi* 9) *ù za-ku-nim* 10) *iš-tu muḫḫi* ^{I}*I-ḫi-ya-na* 11) *ù iš-tu muḫḫi*

[31] Determinative of masculine personal name—scribal error.

mârē^M^-*šu* 12) *za-ki amêlum*^lum^ *iš-tu muḫḫi amêlum*^lum^ 13) *ma-am-ma mi-im-ma* 14) *amêlum*^lum^ *a-na muḫḫi amêlum*^lum^ 15) *la-a i-ra-gu-um* 16) *ša di-na iṣ-but-mi* 17) *1 bilat kaspē*^M^ 18) *ù 1 li-im ḫurā[ṣi]* 19) *a-na šarri*^ri^ *i-din* 20) *ù bît-šu eqlāt*^M^-*šu* 21) *a-na aḫi-šu* 22) ^aban^*kunukku ša šarri.*

"5) *Iḫiyanu*, son of *Sinaranu* 6–8) divided plots of land (allotments) to his brothers. 9) And they are freed (lit. "pure") from *Iḫiyanu* and 11) from his sons. 12) Everybody is free from everybody. 13) Nobody shall raise demands 14) to anybody 15) about somebody. 16) (If someone) raises a legal case, 17) 1 talent of silver 18) and 1000 (sheqels) gold 19) he shall give to the king. 20) And his house, his fields 21) (shall go over) to his brother. 22) The seal of the king."

We see from this text, that the division of property took place between the brothers of a wealthy family. It is important to note that *Iḫiyanu*, possibly the elder brother, divided the plots between his brothers. (There were at least three brothers in all.) Thus, this is a case of the division of a patronymy after the death of the father.

3. U, V, 7 (RS. 17.36).

1) *iš-tu*$_4$ *ûmi*^mi^ *an-ni-i* 2) *a-na pa-ni* ^amelM^*šîbūti*^Mti^ 3) ^I^*A-ba-zu-ya ši-im-ti bîti*^ti^-*šu i-ši-im* 4) *a-nu-ma i-na eqli*^M^: *ra-ba-ti* 5) *ištên*^en^ *ikû eqli a-na rabû* ^I^*Abdi-i-li ad-din-šu* 6) *ù bîtu-ya eqlu*^M^-*ya* 7) *gab-ba mim-mu-ya* 8) *a-na bi-ri* ^I^*Abdi-i-li* 9) *bi-ri* ^I^*Uz-zi-na* 10) *ša-ni-tam šum-ma* ^I^*Abdi-i-li* 11) *ṭup-pa ša-na-a it-ta-ši* 12) *1 li-im kaspu eli-šu* (Lines 13–17 names the four witnesses and the scribe).

"1) From the present day, 2) before witnesses 3) *Abazuya* fixed the fate of his house.[32] 4) "So from my large field 5) one *iku* of field I give my elder (son) *Abdiili*. 6) And my house, my fields, 7) all that I possess, 8) between *Abdiili* 9) (and) between *Uzzinu* (I divide). 10) Further: If *Abdiili* 11) produces another tablet,[33] 12) 1000 (sheqels) of silver to him (to his father he shall pay)."

We learn from this text that the elder son received a personal gift before the division of the father's land and property. It is interesting since it is in accordance with § 165 of the Code of Hammurapi, where the father had the right to give the eldest son a gift, and the other part of his inheritance had to be divided between all sons equally.

4. U, V, 8 (RS. 17.30). This damaged text also seems to be a document concerning the division of an inheritance between the sons of a certain *Abimilku*, son of *[x]* (^I^*A-bi-milku mâr [?])*. At least one of the sons received a slave *(ardu)* and the expression, V'5) *i-na be-ri 3 mârē*^M^-*[šu*

[32] *šimtu* here is not "price," but "the fate," contrary to *J. Nougayrol*, U, V, p. 11.
[33] Changes the conditions of the contract.

(?)] 6') *rabû*[bi] *ki-ma rabūti-šu [. . .]* . . . . ("between [his] three sons 6') the elder one, according to his seniority [. . .]") seems to confirm that this document is similar to the previous one.

5. U, V, 83 (RS. 20.146). This text is also only partly legible:

1) *iš-tu* $_2$*û[m]i an-ni-i-im* 2) *a-na pa-ni* [amelM]*ši-bu-ti* 3) [I]*Kur-wa-na a-kán-na iq-ta-bi* 4) *ma-a* [I]*Nu-me-nu* [I]*Nu-ri-nu* [I]*Abdi-ili* 5) *mârē*[M]*-ya ù [. . .]*

"1) From the present d[a]y 2) before witnesses: 3) *Kurwana* declared the following: 4) "Concerning *Numenu*, *Nurinu* and *Abdiili*, 5) my sons [. . .]" From line 6, which is damaged, it is possible to understand that *Numenu* and *Nurinu* had, in one case, 7) *1 me[-a]t kas[p]a*[M] *u-ma-al-[li]* 8) *i-[n]a qâti aḫḫe*[M]*-šu* 9) *ù* [ṣu[b]at]*n[aḫlapta-šu]* 10) *[i-n]a* [is]*sú-qi-ri i-šak-kan* 11) *[ù] it-te-ṣi a-na sú-qi.* ("7) to repay 100 (sheqels) of silver 8) to his brothers and his clothing 9) [on] the jamb he may put 10) [and] he went to the street.") This was the Ugaritic formula depriving a person of property. Lines 11–17, which are damaged, still allow us to recognize, *kasap*[M] *aš[ša]t Numena* ("the silver of the wife of *Numenu*") as *ka[s]ap aš[š]at* [I]*N[u-rina(?)* ("the silver of the wife of *Nurinu?*"), and also mentions a "house" *(bît)* and "field" *(eqlu)*. Therefore, it seems that this text also is a document about the division of property, and it also deals with patronymic traditions.

6. PRU, VI, 40 (RS. 17.360). This tablet, composed in the presence of the scribe, *Munaḫimu*, seems to date from the time of *Ammistamru* II.[34] Unfortunately, the text is damaged.[35] We learn only that it was composed in the "presence of witnesses," and that a certain 4) [I]*Uk-te-[xx]* did something with 100 sheqels of silver and "the house of [his ?] father" (5) *bît a-bi[-šu?]*). Probably, it was a division of property with his brothers, for he had, in a certain case, 22) *3 me-at k[aspa] a-na qâti aḫḫ[ē*[M]*-šu . . .]* ("22) (to pay) 300 sheqels of silver to [his] brother[s]").

7. PRU, VI, 50. (RS. 17.388).

1) *iš-tu ûmi*[M] *a[-na-]ti(?)* 2) *a-na pa-ni* [amel]*ši-bu-ti* 3) [I]*A-kut-te-nu* 4) *ù* [I]*A-mi-ya-nu* 5) *ù* [I]*Bu-ra-ka-nu aḫi-šu* 6) *ú-za-ki* [I]*Tu-tu aḫi-šu-nu* 7) *20 kaspa e-na-da-ni* 8) [I]*Tu-[t]u* 9) *i-na* [I]*A-ku-te-nu* 10) *ù i[-na]* [I]*A-mi-ya-n[a]* 11) *ù i-na* [[I]]*Bu-r[a]-k[a-na]* 12) *ù ú-za-ki* [I]*T[u]-t[u]* 13) *iš-tu aḫi-šu a-da-[ri-ti]* 14) *šumma ú-ra ši-r[a]* 15) *e-te-e-ru a-na libbi*[bi]*-šu-nu* 16) *ù te-ṣa-bi-tum* [I]*Tu-tu* 17) *50 kaspa ú-ma-la-e* 18) *i-na qâti* [I]*Tu-tu* 19) *50 kaspa ú-ma-la-e i-[na qâti-šu(??)]* 20) *ù Tu-tu u-[x(?)-]z[a](?)-[ki(?)].*

---

[34] *J. Nougayrol*, PRU, VI, p. 41.

[35] Cf. also, the badly damaged PRU, VI, 49 (RS. 17.378A).

"1) From the [pre]sent day 2) before witnesses: 3) *Akuttenu* 4) and *Amiyanu* 5) and *Burakanu* his brother 6) freed (lit. "purified") *Tutu*, their brother.[36] 7) 20 (sheqels) of silver they gave (them) (?).[37] 8) *Tutu* 9) from *Akutenu* 10) and [fro]m *Amiyan[u]* 11) and from *Buraq[anu]*[38] 12) and they freed *Tu[u]t[u]* 13) from their brothers (?)[39] forever.[40] 14) If in future[41] (if) 15) they shall return[42] to their decision (= change their mind) 16) and they shall seize[43] *Tutu*, 17) they shall pay 50 (sheqels) of silver 18) to *Tutu*. 19) 50 (sheqels) of silver they shall pay to him 20) and *Tutu* is fr[ee]d."

The scribe responsible for this tablet, *(šîbu* ^{I}*Abi-malku* ^{amel}*ṭup-pu-ša-ru)* "27) witness, *Abimalku* the scribe,"[44] showed a total ignorance of correct Akkadian, perhaps as a result of Ugaritic or Hurrian influence. Nevertheless, we see that three brothers excluded their brother, *Tutu*, from those people who had the right to divide the family property. The latter received 20 sheqels as compensation for his refusal to participate further in the common household. The three brothers remained with their collective household.

One of the texts given above, PRU, III, 16.129, which concerns the division of property by brothers who inherited the property of their father's house jointly, mentions privileges of the elder son. This included the privilege of disinheriting one son or brother. This is not in the form of a testament, but is a real act with immediate validity. The names of the villages where the lands and other property were located are not given. Perhaps it was of no purpose to mention these location since this type of document did not concern landsale, in which the purchaser would need a more exact definition of the confines of his possession. Here we are dealing with family property and a legal act inside the family, well within

---

[36] We have to understand this as meaning that all the three persons were brothers of *Tutu*.

[37] Instead of *inadinū-šu*, "they gave him."

[38] It is impossible to agree with the translation of J. Nougayrol, "a(!) *Akkutenu*, et a(!) *Ammiyanu*, et a(!) *Burak[anu]*," "to(!) *Akkutenu* and to(!) *Ammiyanu* and to(!) *Burak[anu]*." *Tutu* was not the person who had to pay, it seems that *ina* ("to, into") is here by error instead of *ištu* ("from").

[39] *aḫi-šu*, lit. "his brother," instead of *aḫḫe*^{M}*-šu*.

[40] *a-da-[ri-ti]*, spoiled spelling of *a-di da-ri-ti*.

[41] *ur-ram še-ram*, lit. "tomorrow (and) the day after tomorrow," in the sense of "in future." This was a generally accepted formula in hundreds of legal texts from Ugarit, in this case *u-ra si-ra* is a spoiled spelling.

[42] *e-te-e-ru*, instead of *u-ta-ar-ru*.

[43] Here "you shall seize" in bad orthography.

[44] Instead of *tupšarru, tupušarru;* cf. the same opinion on the half-illiterate scribe, *Rainey*, IOS, III, 1973, p. 39.

known and legally recognized limits. The documents were not composed in the presence of the king, or in the name of the king, or sealed by the king's, or any other official's, seal. On the contrary, they are composed only "before witnesses." This proves that they are not documents concerning royal servicemen, but they involve people who had their land in the villages, the rural communities of the kingdom. Naturally, only new conditions were mentioned, i.e., those connected with the results of the division of the inheritance, or the disinheritance of certain persons. Therefore, the well-known and traditional obligatory taxes, corvée, etc., were not mentioned at all.

Four brothers seems to have been the maximum in one large patronymic family. In the specific conditions of Ugarit large patronymies could not survive for a very long time. This conclusion is by no means in contradiction to the comparison of landsale documents given above. Thus, the general conclusion derived from the texts presented in this chapter is that the family in Ugarit was not a large one, and had relatively few members.

The Preference Given to the Family to Regain its Land

This problem is of importance in understanding various trends in landholding, concerning certain families and their privileges in regard to their former land.

U, V, 6 (RS. 17.149). 0) ^{I}*Mu-na-ḫi-mu* ^{amel}*ṭupšarru* 1) *iš-tu ûmi*^{miKAM} *an-ni-i-im* 2) *a-na pa-ni*^{M} ^{amelM}*šîbūti*^{M} 3) ^{Iil}*Rašap-a-bu ù* ^{f}*Pi-id-da aššat-su* 4) *il-te-qú-ni 4 ikâ eqla*^{M} 5) *qa-du* ^{iṣ}*serdi-šu* 6) *qa-du ardūti*^{M}*-šu qa-du UGULA*^{MEŠ}*-šu (= aklišu)*[44a] 7) *i-na eqli*^{M} *Ṣa-a-i* 8) *iš-tu* ^{I}*Ya-ri-ma-na mâr Ḫu-za-mi* 9) *i-na 4 me-at kaspi*^{M} 10) *eqlu*^{M} ^{iṣ}*serdu* 11) *ṣa-ma-ad i-na* ^{il}*Šamšu ûmi*^{mi} 12) *a-na Rašap-a-bi ù* 13) *a-na* ^{f}*Pi-id-da aššati-šu* 14) *ù a-na mârē*^{M}*-šu-nu a-di* 15) *da-ri du-ri šum-ma ur-ra*16)*-am še-ra-am* ^{I}*Ya-ri-ma-nu* 17) *ù mârē*^{M}*-šu i-tù-ur-ni* 18) *a-n[a] libbi*^{bi}*-šu-nu 1 li-im kaspu* 19) *eli-šu-nu ù eqlu*^{M} *a-na* ^{Iil}*Rašap-a-bi* 20) *ù a-na* ^{f}*Pi-id-da* 21) *ù šum-ma* ^{Iil}*Rašap-a-bu ù aššat-su* 22) *i-tù-ur-ni a-na libbi-šu-nu* 23) *ù k[i]-šu-ma šu-nu-ma ša-ni-tam* 24) *[pa-na-]na-ma eqlu an-nu-ù ša* ^{I}*I-za-al-da* 25) *a-bi* ^{f}*Pi-id-du ù i-na-an-na* 26) *eqlu*^{M} *i-tù-ur eqil*^{M}[44b] 27) ^{f}*Pi-id-da ù [*^{Iil}*Rašap](?)-a-bu.*

[44a] *qa-du UGULA*^{MEŠ}*-šu* seen on the autograph (Pl. II) given by *P. R. Berger*, UF, I, 1969, p. 121.

[44b] *Nougayrol—a-[n]a?*, *Berger*, UF, I, 1969, p. 121, *A. [ŠA]MEŠ.*

"0) *Munaḫimu*, the scribe. . . . 1) From the present day 2) before witnesses: 3) *Rašapabu* and *Pidda*, his wife 4) bought 4 *iku* of field 5) together with its olive trees, 6) together with its slaves, together with their overseers, 7) located among the fields of (the village) *Ṣau*, 8) from *Yarimanu*, son of *Ḫuzamu* 9) for 400 (sheqels) of silver. 10) The field, the olive trees 11) are in possession like daylight 12) of *Rašapabu* and 13) of *Pidda*, his wife 14) and of their sons 15) forever. If in 16) future *Yarimanu* 17) and his sons shall return 18) to their decision (change their minds), 1000 (sheqels) of silver 19) shall be on them[45] and the field (belongs) to *Rašapabu* 20) and to *Pidda*. 21) And if *Rašapabu* and his wife 22) return on their decision (change their minds) 23) so it is according to their (decision).[46] Further: 24) [Form]erly this field belonged to *Izalda*, 25) the father of *Pidda* and now 26) the field returns. The fi[eld]s are of 27) *Pidda* and *[Rašap]abu*."

This document is of extraordinary interest. The land transaction is a normal one, but there is an indication that the motivation of *Rašapabu* and his wife, *Pidda*, in purchasing the land was to regain the property formerly belonging to *Yzalda*, *Pidda's* father. This shows that *Pidda* was given preference in the purchase of this land. The situation could have been the following: *Yzalda* had to sell his land, the property of his family. His heirs had the privilege to buy it back before other purchasers.[47] Perhaps, *Yzalda* had no male heirs and thus this right passed to *Pidda*. This act of purchase returned the land to the legal heir. The document was not composed in the presence of the king or other royal authorities. Thus, also here we have an internal issue of the rural community of *Ṣaᶜu*. The text is also very important in seeing a tendency to maintain the stability of land-property within the community.

---

[45] I.e., *Yarimanu* and his sons had to pay 1,000 shekels of silver to *Rašapabu* and *Pidda*.

[46] That means that *Rašapabu* and *Pidda* had the right to decide freely and to change their decision, without paying any fine.

[47] The Eshnunna Laws § 38. If one of the brothers sells his share and his brother wants to buy it, the latter must pay in full the average (price) of another. § 39 is even more important, where, if a man became impoverished and sold his house, the day the buyer will sell the former owner of the house may redeem (*R. Yaron*, The Laws of Eshnunna, Jerusalem, 1969, pp. 40–41).

GENERAL CONCLUSIONS

In summing up all the evidence we may say that large families, i.e. patronymies, sometimes existed in Ugarit. But the general trend was towards its disintegration, and the large majority of families were small ones. We know of no patronymy which remained undivided into the third generation. Most of the families divided property according to the testament of the father, or it came into effect between the brothers.

It is difficult to discover all the reasons why this process took place in Ugarit. But, it may be that the maritime position of the kingdom, its commercial role in the ancient Near East during the XIV–XIII centuries b.c., and the fact that Ugarit was in the focus of the political, cultural and economic influences of Hittite Asia Minor, Mesopotamia, Egypt and the Aegean world, could have spurred the more rapid development of its society.

If we take, for purposes of comparison, the more or less contemporary societies of Alalaḫ (Mukish) and Arrapḫa (Nuzu), situated inland, and very far from the commercial routes and activities (as was Arrapḫa particularly) we see that in their societies patronymies, and more patriarchal societies in general, flourished.[48]

Our investigation also makes it clear that the primary unit inside the rural community was the individual family, the "house(hold)," *bîtu/bt (É)*.

Naturally, full understanding of the society of Ugarit needs additional investigation concerning the social status of the royal dependents (servicemen), *bnš mlk*, royal real estate, the economy, organization of craftsmanship, and other issues. But the principal socio-economic unit in Ugarit was the rural community, and the wealth of the kingdom was based on its productivity.

There is no parallel, among any other ancient Oriental societies, situated in the unirrigated zone, to the abundance of documentation from ancient Ugarit. Thus, conclusions concerning Ugarit also have a certain value in reconstructing the socio-economic history of other countries for which the documentary evidence is scarce.

---

[48] *N. B. Yankovskaya*, Zemlevladeniye bolshesemeynych domovych obshtshin v klinopisnych istochnikach (Landownership of Large Patronymies, According to Cuneiform Sources), VDI, 1959, No. 1, pp. 35–51 (Russian); *N. B. Yankovskaya*, Zur Geschichte der hurritischen Gesellschaft (Auf Grund von Rechtsurkunden aus *Arrapḫa* und *Alalaḫ*), "Abstracts of the XXV International Congress of Orientalists," Moscow, 1960 (1062), I, pp. 226–32; *N. B. Yankovskaya*, Communal Self-government and the King of the State of *Arrapḫa*, JESHO, 12, 1969, pp. 233–82; *M. Dietrich, O. Loretz*, Die Soziale Struktur von *Alalaḫ* und *Ugarit* (IV) Die *É* = *bîtu*-Listen aus *Alalaḫ* IV als Quelle für Erforschung der gesellschaftlichen Schichtung von *Alalaḫ* im 15. Jh. v. Chr., ZA, 60, 1970, pp. 88–123.

Appendix I

Royal Landownership

Texts U, V, 159 (RS. 17.86), 160 (RS. 17.102), and U, V, 161 (RS. 17.325), given above, concern land purchases made by the queen, in this case, the queen-mother of Ugarit. The fact of the purchase is very significant since it denies the theory, until now unproven, that in the ancient Near East the king was the owner of all lands in his kingdom. If such were the case, then land purchase by the king (or queen) would be inexplicable. We see from the texts, that the queen had to perform all the formalities required of any other citizen who purchased land. Thus, even if only formally, the king was not the only real landowner of the kingdom. He was only the sovereign in the political sense, and had the right to receive the lands of the *nayyālu*, or debtors taken into slavery abroad (PRU, IV, 17.130 above). Only the lands of the royal real estate and of the land fund, distributed to royal servicemen, were at the king's full disposal. Such a view conflicts with the point of view of A. F. Rainey, who regards the kings as the feudal lords of all lands in the kingdom.[1]

[1] *Rainey*, A Social Structure, pp. 32–36.

Appendix II

Demographic Survey of the Population of the Rural Communities of Ugarit

It would be very interesting to know how large the population of the rural communities was in the kingdom of Ugarit in the XIV–XIII centuries b.c. Naturally, such an attempt can only be a rough approximation. First, we have to take into account that the various countries of the ancient Near East differed in density of population. Of course, population density was greater in the irrigated areas.

The works available in this field are based on specific calculations related to the character of the sources used in each case.[1] Thus, they cannot

[1] *I. M. Diakonoff*, Obshtshestvenny i gosudarstvenny stroi drevnevo Dvurechya, Shumer, Moscow, 1959, pp. 9–39 (Russian), pp. 291–92 (English summary); *V. V. Struve*, Gosadarstvo Lagash, Moscow, 1961, pp. 3–57 (Russian); *I. M. Diakonoff*,

be used as examples in our study. We must base our calculations on the interpretation of the Ugaritic sources available. These include conscription lists, tax lists, lists of villages, arms delivery lists, as well as texts which indicate the average size of the Ugaritic family (cf. below).

The length of the coast of Ugarit reached approximately sixty kilometers. That was the maximum depth of the inland territory as well.[2] Thus, the maximum territory occupied by Ugarit was 3,000–4,000 square kilometers. There were also mountainous areas as well as forested areas.[3] Some of the villages can be localized[4] more or less exactly. As shown in Table No. 1, there were approximately 190 villages. This figure appears to be convincing. Thus, we may assume that there were approximately 180–200 villages existing at any one time.

We have no proof that even those texts concerning the distribution of various taxes, payments, and duties between the members of the village communities (cf. Ch. II), list all the households of the community—even when the texts are complete. It is possible that some households had to perform one obligation and others different obligations. However, it seems realistic to assume that the texts relating to military conscription covered the whole community, mobilizing the heads of families, or adults from every household.

Text CTC, 71, discussed in Chapter II, as well as PRU, III, 11.841, concern only a small scale conscription of the villagers at the same time that texts CTC, 119 (UT, 321), PRU, V, 16 (UT, 2016), and PRU, VI 95 (RS. 19.74) give us the figures for a general conscription. (Villages for whom the figures are broken have been omitted.)

1. PRU, VI, 95, 12	*Ẓrn*/[al]*Za-ri-nu*	13 people
2. PRU, VI, 95, 13	*Art*/[al]*A-ru-tu*	13 people
3. PRU, VI, 95, 4	*Ṯlrby*/[al]*Šal-lir$_x$-ba-a*	10 people

Razvitiye zemelnych otnosheniyi v Assiri'i, Leningrad, 1949, pp. 79–90 (Russian); *W. F. Albright*, The Amarna Letters from Palestine, Syria the Philistines and Phoenicia, CAH, Ch. II, XXIII, 1961, p. 19—200,000 inhabitants of Palestine in the late Bronze Age.

[2] *J. Nougayrol*, PRU, IV, p. 17; *G. Buccellati*, Cities and Nations of Ancient Syria, Rome, 1967, p. 38.

[3] Cf. PRU, III, 11.700, where the total of the text is designated as 3) *âlāni* DIDLI *ḫuršāni* ("the villages of the mountain district").

[4] *M. Astour*, Place-Names from the Kingdom of Alalaḫ in the North Syrian List of Thutmose IV; A Study in Historical Topography, JNES, XXII, 1963, pp. 220–41; *M. Astour*, Ma'ḫadu, the Harbour of Ugarit, JESHO, XIII, 1970, No. 2, p. 112ff.; *J.-C. Courtois*, Deux villes du royaume d'Ugarit dans la valée du Nahr-el-Kebir en Syria du Nord, "Syria," XL, 1963, pp. 261–73; *J. Nougayrol*, Soukas-Shuksu, "Syria," XXXVIII, 1961, p. 215, etc.

4. PRU, VI, 95, 6	*Šlmy*/^{al}*Šal-ma-a*	5 people
5. PRU, VI, 95, 5	*Ṯmry*/^{al}*Šam-ra-a*	6 people
6. CTC, 119, II, 1–12	*Arny*	10 people
7. CTC, 119, I, 25–48	*Mᶜrby*	21 people
8. CTC, 119, III, 1–46; IV, 1–19	*Ubrᶜy*	61 people
9. CTC, 119, II, 13–20	*Mᶜr*	6 people
10. CTC, 119, I, 12–24	*Ulm*	21 people
11. CTC, 119, II, 21–29	*Bqᶜt*	7 people
12. CTC, 119, II, 34–37	*Ḫlb Rpš*	3 people
13. CTC, 119, II, 35–39	*Rkby*	3 people
14. CTC, 119, II, 40–49	*Šᶜrt*	8 people
15. PRU, V, 16	*Miḫd*	at least 90 people
Total for 15 villages		277 people

We arrive at an average figure, for one village, of 18.5 persons. This is the average number to be conscripted from a single village. Thus, the total number of men conscripted on the occassion of a mobilization would have been: $180 \times 18.5 = 3{,}330$—$200 \times 18.5 = 3{,}600$.

We have only one indirect way to prove the accuracy of these figures. This is by means of the texts concerning taxes and other duties, which indicate, like the conscription texts, a certain proportion between the villages responsible for providing a small number of men, and those responsible for providing a large number of men, i.e. between smaller and bigger villages. Table No. 4 compares the tax lists with the conscription texts.[5]

Thus, it seems that the nine texts, and the data from Table No. 2, where information about the grain tithe was calculated, prove that we can generally accept the division of the villages into three groups according to the numbers of conscripted men from each.

It must be noted, that CTC, 67 and PRU, III, 11.800 give only figures dealing with the villages of the third group—the small villages. CTC, 68 shows figures for the second group (middle-size villages), larger than for the first group, and the amount of grain from *Šᶜrt* (group II) exceeds that of group I also.

On the other hand, texts PRU, III, 10.044, 11.790, and PRU, V, 58 mention several villages whose figures exceed those of the large villages of group I. This fact must not be ignored.

[5] Cf. *Liverani*, Cammunantés . . . pp. 151–52, where the first steps towards the use of the data from Alalaḫ for demographic statistics are used.

Table No. 4

1	Names of the villages	Average of conscripted men in the group of villages	CTC, 65 (UT, 108)[4]	CTC, 67 (UT, 110)[5]	CTC, 68 (UT, 65)[6]	CTC, 71 (UT, 113)[7]	PRU, III, 10.044[10]	PRU, III, 11.790[12]	PRU, III, 11.800[13]	PRU, V, 58 (UT, 2058)[16]	PRU, V, 74 (UT, 2074)[18]	Results of Table No. 2—grain tax[19]
1	2	3	4	5	6	7	8	9	10	11	12	13
1	*Miḫd*	—	—	—	—	—	—	—	—	—	—	—
2	*Ubr*^{c}*y*	75.5[1]	5	—	3	2	18 *kùr* grain + 1 ox + X	14	?[14]	130	—	18
3	*Ẓrn*		—	—	—	1		—	—	—	—	10
4	*Art*		—	—	—	1		—	—	—	—	6.25
5	*Arny*	13.7[2]	1	—	—	½[8]	2 *kùr*[11] grain, 6.5 oxen	—	—	20	2	2
6	*Ṯlrby*		—	—	—	1		—	—	—	—	5
7	*M*^{c}*rby*		—	—	5	1		1	—	?[17]	2	—
8	*Ulm*		2	—	6	—		—	—	—	2	—
9	*Š*^{c}*rt*		—	—	—	—		—	—	24	2	105
10	*Šlmy*		—	—	—	⅓[9]	—	—	—	?[12]	—	—
11	*Ṯmry*		—	—	—	1		—	—	?[17]	—	6
12	*M*^{c}*r*	5.5[3]	1	—	—	½[8]		2	9	8[17]	1	—
13	*Bq*^{c}*t*		1	6	—	—		2	—	—	—	—
14	*Ḫlb-rpš*		1	14	—	—		2	—	—	1	—
15	*Rkby*		—	—	—	—		—	2	—	—	—
Villages paying more, than group I							50 *kùr* grain 13(?) oxen *Bekani*	30 *Bekani*[15]	400[15]			50 *Bekani*

[1] Large villages.
[2] Middle-size villages.
[3] Small villages.

At least one village from every group has statistics available for eight of the ten possible categories (= 80 percent of the texts available). At the same time, the special group in which the figure is higher is mentioned only three (four ?) times. We may conclude that the largest villages appeared only in one-third of the given texts, i.e., less than forty percent of the texts. If one of the fifteen villages is $^{1}/_{15}$ of the total, then the infrequent mention of the large villages shows that their number could not have exceeded $^{1}/_{30}$–$^{1}/_{45}$ = $^{1}/_{40}$. If we assume that the population in such villages was twice that of the large group, then we could estimate an average of 150 families per village.

Text CTC, 65 mentions nine villages. The figures show that:

Group I	—	2 villages	=	23%
Group II	—	2 villages	=	23%
Group III	—	5 villages	=	54%
				100%

CTC, 67 mentions twelve villages. Only one of these villages *(Šḥq)* paid twenty-four jars of wine, i.e., twice the amount paid by the villages of Group III. Thus, we have the following figures:

Group II	—	1 village	=	8%
Group III	—	11 villages	=	92%
				100%

---

[4] List of villages which performed a certain number of days of labour-corvée (cf. Ch. II, pp. 24–25).

[5] List of vine tax (cf. Ch. II pp. 40–42).

[6] The object listed is not clear.

[7] Partial conscription list of bowmen (cf. Ch. II, pp. 18–19).

[8] *Arny* and *M*^{c}*r* together contributed one person.

[9] *Ykn*^{c}*m*, *Šlmy* and *Ull* together contributed one bowman.

[10] Taxes paid in wine, oxen and grain.

[11] One or two villages; the name of the second village was not preserved.

[12] Duties of the "mountain district."

[13] The real object of the tax or duty is not precisely known, but it was probably corvée counted in days(?).

[14] Figure-sign broken.

[15] The largest number, 50, from ^{al}*Ma-qa-bu;* but we have no basis for comparison with the large villages.

[16] Cf. Ch. II, pp. 31–33; tax-list of the Hittite king.

[17] Illegible figures.

[18] Figure-signs preserved partly; purpose of the list is unknown.

[19] Average payments in *kùr*'s.

CTC, 68 mentions ten villages. Of these:

Group I	—	2 villages	=	20%
Group II	—	8 villages	=	80%
				100%

In CTC, 71, the figures are preserved for forty-one villages.

Group I	—	(2 persons for 1 village)	3 villages	=	8%
Group II	—	(1 persons for 1 village)	19 villages	=	46%
Group III	—	(1 persons for 2–3 villages)	19 villages	=	46%
					100%

In text PRU, III, 10.044 figures are preserved for fifteen villages.

Large villages	—	1 village	=	7%
Group I	—	4 villages	=	26%
Group II	—	7 villages	=	47%
Group III	—	3 villages	=	20%
				100%

In text PRU, III, 11.790 figures for thirty-three villages are preserved.

Large villages	—	1 village	=	3%
Group I	—	4 villages	=	12%
Group II	—	13 villages	=	40%
Group III	—	15 villages	=	45%
				100%

In text PRU, III, 11.800 figures are preserved for twenty-five villages.

Group I	—	3 villages	=	11%
Group II	—	12 villages	=	41%
Group III	—	14 villages	=	48%
				100%

In text PRU, V, 58 figures for fourty-four villages are preserved.

Large villages	—	1 village	=	2%
Group I	—	6 villages	=	14%
Group II	—	12 villages	=	27%
Group III	—	25 villages	=	57%
				100%

In text PRU, V, 74 figures for twenty-seven villages are preserved.

Group I	—	(more than the figure 2 concerned)	6 villages	=	23%
Group II	—	(2 concerned.)	9 villages	=	33%
Group III	—	(1 concerned.)	12 villages	=	44%
					100%

We may take, in addition, the data derived from various small texts:

Payments from large villages—

	(more than 25 *kùr*)	5 villages	=	19%
Group I	(15–25 *kùr*)	4 villages	=	15%
Group II	(7–14 *kùr*)	3 villages	=	11%
Group III	(1–6 *kùr*)	15 villages	=	55%
				100%

These figures help us calculate the role of various groups of villages in the general demographic picture of the villages of the kingdom.

Text	Large Villages	Group I	Group II	Group III
		(Percentages according to the single texts and Table No. 2)		
1. CTC, 65	—	23	23	54
2. CTC, 67	—	—	8	92
3. CTC, 68	—	20	80	—
4. CTC, 71	—	8	46	46
5. PRU, III, 10.044	7	26	47	20
6. PRU, III, 11.790	3	12	40	45
7. PRU, III, 11.800	—	11	44	45
8. PRU, V, 58	2	14	27	57
9. PRU, V, 74	2	23	33	44
10. Table No. 2[1]	19	15	11	55
	31:10 =	156:10 =	359:10 =	958:10 =
	3%	15%	36%	46% = 100%

[1] Including 10.044.

These figures are only approximations, but they may not be very far from reality. If, in basing further calculation on them, and assuming the figure of 180–200 villages, we remove the following groups:

1) Large villages	1,8–2 × 3	=	5–6 villages
2) Group I	1,8–2 × 15	=	27–30 villages
3) Group II	1,8–2 × 36	=	65–72 villages
4) Group III	1,8–2 × 46	=	83–92 villages
	100%	=	180–200 villages

Taking into account the tentative average of mobilized men in every group of villages we receive the following number of people.

1) Large villages	5–6 × 150	=	750–900
2) Group I	17–30 × 75.5	=	2038–2265
3) Group II	65–72 × 13.7	=	890–986
4) Group III	83–92 × 5	=	415–460
			4093–4611

Thus, an average figure would be:

$4093 + 4611 = 8704 : 2 = 4352$ men mobilized at the general mobilizations from the villages of Ugarit. This differs from the previously calculated figure of 3330–3600 = 3465 persons. Thus, the number could have been between 3465–4352 ≈ 3906 men.

The largest conscription text, PRU, V, 16, where all the individuals are referred to only as *bn X*, "son of x (the father's name)," allows us to conclude that only the heads of the families were named, or only one man from every family. This forces us to conclude that the conscription texts listed only people subdued to military conscription, not elderly persons or invalids. The number of men listed could not exceed 15–20% of all adult men, taking into account a relatively short lifespan. Thus, their number could be not more than 600–800. Taking 700 as an average, the number of adult free-born villagers may have been approximately 4100–4700 (an average of 4400). But, in order to be more exact, we must take into account the size of the average family.

Texts PRU, V, 44, PRU, II, 80, and CTC, 81 were analyzed and reconstructed in Chapter VII. Using these texts, we can get an approximate idea of average family size. The figures arrived at are only approximations because of the bad state of preservation of these texts.

1) *Ḫzmtn*, 2 sons, 1 wife	=	4 persons
2) *Swn*, 1 son, 1 wife, 1 brother	=	4 persons
3) *Pln*, 2 sons, 1 x (?)	=	4 persons (at least)
4) *Ymrn*, 1 wife, 1 son	=	3 persons
5) *Prd*, 1 wife, 1 son	=	3 persons
6) *Prṯ*, 2 x, 1 wife	=	4 persons
7) *ᶜdyn*, 1 wife, 2 sons	=	4 persons (at least)
8) *Anntn*, 1 wife, 2 sons, 1 x (?)	=	5 persons (at least)
9) *Aǵltn*, 1 wife, 1 son	=	3 persons
10) *[x]ḏmu*, 1(?) x, 1 son, 1 wife	=	4 persons (at least)
11) *Ydln*, 1 wife, 2 sons	=	4 persons
12) *Ṯmgdl*, 1 wife, 1 son	=	3 persons
13) *Annḏr*, 1 wife, 1 son	=	3 persons
14) *Nrn*, 1 wife(?), 2 sons + x	=	5 persons (at least)
15) *Plzn*, 1 wife(?), 1 son, 1 daughter-in-law	=	4 persons
16) *Bᶜly*, 1 wife, 1 son(?), 1 daughter + x	=	4 persons
17) *Bᶜlsip*, 1 wife(?), 1 son, 1 daughter-in-law	=	4 persons
18) *Nrn*, 1 wife(?), + x, 2 sons	=	4 persons (at least)
19) *Ṯlḫny*, 1 wife(?), 3 sons, 3 daughter-in-law	=	8 persons (at least)
Total		77 persons (+ x)

If we assume that there was at least one additional person in 8 of the families, and we take half of this number as certain, we have 4 additional persons, for a total of 81 persons in 19 families. As it was pointed out in Chapter VII, no children were mentioned in these texts. The number of children might have reached ⅓ of the number calculated above. Thus, there may have been up to 27 minor children in these families. (This small number of children has been reached by taking into account the high mortality rate; it is a minimum number.) Thus, there were approximately 108 persons among the 19 families = 5.7 persons per family.

Text PRU, V, 80 (cf. Chapt. VII) mentions workmen who were not freeborn, or who were semi-free. The sizes of the families mentioned in this text are as follows:

1) *Bn. Bᶜln*, 3 workmen, their head, his 4 daughters	=	9 persons
2) *Yrḫm*, 2 sons, 2 workmen, 3 youth, 4 daughters	=	9 persons
3) *bn Lwn*, 6 workmen	=	7 persons
4) *Bn Bᶜly*, 6 workmen, 1 *ḫupšu*, 4 wives (or women)	=	12 persons
5) *Bn Lg*, 2 sons, 2 workmen, 1 sister	=	6 persons
6) *Šty*, 1 son	=	2 persons
Total		45 persons

Here, too, minor children may be added to the total. The percentage of working personnel is high. Therefore the number of children probably did not exceed ¼ of the persons listed here. Thus, the number of children may have reached 11. The total number of people in these families could have been 56 persons = 56 : 6 ≈ 9 persons per family. Not all families had workmen in their possession; those that did were the more wealthy families. They were not numerous among the villages of Ugarit, and do not, therefore, have any great bearing on the total village population. Among the people named in PRU, V, 80, we have 22 workmen. If we divide this number among all the families listed above, we get 1 workingman per family. Thus, it is possible to combine the total of the results received from the 19 families and PRU, V, 80: 108 + 56 = 164. Dividing this total among 25 families (19 + 6), we arrive at an average of 6.5 persons (approximately) per family, including children and unfree or semi-free working personnel.

In order to calculate the general population we must multiply the number of people conscripted by 6.5, the average number of persons in an Ugaritic family. The results are: approximately 3900 × 6.5 ≈ 24,350. We must also add the approximate number of elderly persons reckoned at 700. We thus arrive at an average of 25,000 people making up the population of the villages of Ugarit. We must take into account that this is not the total population of the kingdom. To arrive at this figure we would have to include the population of the town of Ugarit, the royal servicemen *(bnš mlk)*, and other smaller segments of the population.

This data is very preliminary and far from exact. However, it is impossible at present to use any other method to calculate population figures for Ugarit. Future publications will have to demonstrate the correctness or incorrectness of this method, or attempt to improve it.

Appendix III

Chronology of the Late-Ugaritic Period[1]

	Amurru	Ugarit	Ḫatti
1400			
1375	*Aziru*	*Ammistamru I*	*Šuppiluliuma*
		Niqmaddu II	
1350			*Arnuwanda II*
	DU-Tešub	*Arḫalba*	*Mursilis II*
1325	*Duppitešub*	*Niqmepa*	
1300	*Bentešina*		*Muwatallu*
	(Šapili)		
			Urḫitešub
	Bentešina		*Ḫattusilis III*
1275		*Ammistamru II*	
1250	*Šaušgamuwa*		*Tudḫaliya IV*
		Ibiranu	
1225		*Niqmaddu III*	*Arnuwanda III*
		Ḫammurapi	
1200			*Šuppiluliuma II*

[1] This table is given according to *H. Klengel*, Geschichte Syriens im 2. Jahrtausend, v. U.Z., Teil 2, Mittel- und Südsyrien, Berlin, 1969, p. 455.

INDICES

1. Ugaritic and Akkadian texts from Ugarit[1]

CL. 1957, 3 38–39
CL. 1957, 4 44
CTC. 3, V *76*
CTC. 4 76, *76*
CTC. 6 76
CTC. 14 *73*
CTC. 15 75
CTC. 17 *76*
CTC. 65 24, 106, 108–109
CTC. 66 24–25
CTC. 67 41, *61*, 105–106, 108–109
CTC. 68 105–106, 108–109
CTC. 69 31, *31*, 33, *60*
CTC. 70 *31*
CTC. 71 5, *16*, 18; 21, *19*, 32, *60*, *61*, *72*, 104, 106, 108–109
CTC. 79 21
CTC. 81 84–87, 110
CTC. 84 23
CTC. 119 19–21, 104–105
CTC. 136 24, 27

PRU. II, 4 *40*
PRU. II, 5 *40*
PRU. II, 7 *50*
PRU. II, 10 25, 27, 34
PRU. II, 24 *68*, 81
PRU. II, 33 82
PRU. II, 59 28
PRU. II, 68 *20*
PRU. II, 80 84–87, 110
PRU. II, 81 *20*, *60*
PRU. II, 82 92
PRU. II, 84 *29*, *72*
PRU. II, 92 *75*
PRU. II, 93 *82*

[1] About other systems of citation of these texts and their identification according to other citation systems cf. M. Dietrich, O. Loretz, *Konkordanz der ugaritischen Textzählung*, Neukirchen–Vluyn, 1972.

PRU. II, 98 *29*
PRU. II, 101 24
PRU. II, 104 *83*
PRU. II, 106 40
PRU. II, 154 72–73, 75
PRU. II, 161 *78*
PRU. II, 171 33
PRU. II, 173 78
PRU. II, 176 *17*, 31, *31*
PRU. II, 181 *20*, *25*, *60*
PRU. II, 184 *7*
PRU. II, 185 *7*
PRU. II, 186 *7*
PRU. II, 188 *7*
PRU. III, 10.044 *16*, 35–36, 41, 43, 105–106, 108–109
PRU. III, 11.700 *2*
PRU. III, 11.790 *16–17*, 24, *24*, 103–107, 109
PRU. III, 11.800 *47*, *72*, 105–107, 109
PRU. III, 11.830 24–25, *61*
PRU. III, 11.841 *16*, 19, *19*, 21, 104
PRU. III, 15.20 *17*, 44
PRU. III, 15.81 *58*
PRU. III, 15.89 53, 55, 91
PRU. III, 15.90 96
PRU. III, 15.114 *27*, 49
PRU. III, 15.115 *25*
PRU. III, 15.122 *55*
PRU. III, 15.123 91
PRU. III, 15.132 *35*
PRU. III, 15.136 92
PRU. III, 15.137 80
PRU. III, 15.140 61, *61*, *92*
PRU. III, 15.141 55, 61, *61*
PRU. III, 15.142 *61*
PRU. III, 15.143 *92*
PRU. III, 15.145 *55*, 92
PRU. III, 15.147 51
PRU. III, 15.155 61, *61*
PRU. III, 15.156 91, 95
PRU. III, 15.168 55
PRU. III, 15.179 *47*
PRU. III, 15.182 *61*, 94–95
PRU. III, 15.183 *47*
PRU. III, 15.189 *47*

2. Selected Oriental Terms

a) Ugaritic

b. Akkadian

rêšu 55
sākinu, šākinu *17*, *49*, 53–54, 56, *56*, 63–64, 79–80, 82, 83, 94
serdu 42
ṣabū *18*–19, *22*, *59*
ṣibbiru 70–71
sākin ekallim 49–50
šangu 42
šamnu 42
ša šêpe-šu *79*
šarrakuti (var, širku) 31
šatammu 54, *54*
šê 35, 37–38
šennu 44–45
šîbūtu 56, 64, *79–80*, 94, 97–99
šimtu 97
šipru šarri *25*
šikāru 35, *35*
širku 48
tamkāru 33, *34*, 39, 42, 57, *57*, 63, 78, *79*
tappūtu 78
ugula 39
unuššu 53, 55, 90–91
zittu 96

c. Sumerian

DUG 40, 41
DUG GEŠTIN 41
É 102, *102*
GUD 43
ḪU *16*
MAŠKIM *17*, *49*, 56, 82–83
PA 37, 39
SA.GAZ 58
SAG. DU *18*
SÍG *17*
ŠEN.MEŠ *45*
TAL.MEŠ. siparri 44
UDU.NIN.MA 44
URU 7
ZÌ.KAL.MEŠ 36
ZIZ.AN.NA 36

3. Personal Names

a. Written in Ugaritic Cuneiform Alphabet

Abdḫr 22
Ad^{c}y 28
Aḏmn(d) 72
[A]dmu 85, 87
Adty 43
Agpṯn 68
Agpṯr 68
Agyn 86–87
Aġltn 85, 87–88, 110
Aliyn B^{c}l(d) 76
Alkbl 34
Ann 68–69
Ann[d]r 68, 85, 110
Annmn 68
Annt[n] 85, 87, 110
Arkš [ ] 68
Aṯrt (d) 76, *76*
^{c}bdilt 78
^{c}bdyrḫ 43
^{c}dn 22, 28
^{c}dyn 85–86, 110
^{c}br(d) 72
^{c}pṯn 23
^{c}yn 23
B^{c}l *71*
B^{c}ln 89, 111
B^{c}ly 86–87, 89, 110–111
B^{c}lsip 110
Bdn 68
Brqn 79
Brrn 69
Brzn 69
Buly 23
Dml(d) 26, *26*
Dnil 75
Dnn 23
Ḏmry 28
Grb 23
Gyn 68
Hbm 42
Ḥdd 85, 87
Ḥgbn 82
Ḥgby 47
Ḥnn 78

b) Written in Akkadian Cuneiform and Other Scripts